January 18, 2010

To: Brian,

Fair winds!

Charles E. McGee

Tuskegee Airman
The Biography of
Charles E. McGee

Air Force Fighter Combat
Record Holder

By
Charlene E. McGee Smith, Ph.D.

BRANDEN PUBLISHING COMPANY
Boston

Library of Congress Cataloging-in-Publication Data

Smith Charlene E. McGee.
Tuskegee airman : the biography of Charles E. McGee, Air Force fighter combat record holder / by Charlene E. McGee Smith.
    p. cm.
Includes bibliographical references (p.   ) and index.
ISBN 0828320462 (alk. paper.) (Cloth edition)
ISBN 0828321868, ISBN 0780828321860 (Hard edition)
1. McGee, Charles E., 1919- .
2. World War, 1939-1945--Aerial operations, American.
3. World War, 1939-1945--Participation, Afro-American
4. Korean War, 1950-1953--Participation, Afro-American.
5. Vietnamese Conflict, 1961-1975--Participation,
    Afro-American.
6. United States. Army Air Forces--Biography.
7. United States. Air Force--Biography.
8. Afro-American air pilots--Biography.
I. Title.
D790.S5676 1999
951.904'248'092--dc--21   99-18279
[b]   CIP

BRANDEN BOOKS
PO Box 812094 Wellesley MA 02482
Boston

For Mom,
who kept the home fire burning,
and Bill,
who completes me.

Contents:

Acknowledgments

The contribution of family, friends and associates to Dad's story is living testimony of their high regard for him. I am grateful for the role each played in bringing his biography to life. Many sent stories and provided anecdotes from times they shared with him. Some included photos and news clippings as well. However incorporated, every offering added to my insight, understanding and ability to convey events in their fullest sense.

Special acknowledgment goes to my sister, Yvonne, and son, Damon, whose critical eye and editorial comments were invaluable. She challenged me to be specific, provide perspective and hold high standards for quality, and he counseled me to stay focused and tuned to my inner voice.

In the editing department, thanks also go to Theodore W. Robinson, a Tuskegee Airmen and former editor with the Smithsonian Institution, who helped keep aviation facts in context, Louise Mohr for her keen proofreading skill, and my brother Ron, who brought my word processing capabilities into the modern era. Ron joined Dad, Yvonne and me for a week long edit session in October, 1997, after which the project gained direction and momentum.

I appreciate the aid of Gillian Berckowitz, Senior Editor of the Ohio University (O.U.) Press, who offered pointers to help me navigate in the unfamiliar territory of commercial publishing; Gary Kirksey, Assistant Professor in the O.U. School for Visual Communication, for Dad's Studio Portrait and other photographic assistance; Dr. Hubertus L. Bloemer, Chair of Geography and Director of the Cartographic Center at O.U., who provided maps for chapters on military campaigns; and

6 Charlene Smith

Harvey McCormick, Tuskegee Airman and longtime friend of Dad, for his assistance with indexing.

While this work was in creation, perhaps the greatest sacrifice was made by William and my youngest daughter, Charon, who gave up wife and mother more often than they would have liked. Thanks for loving me enough to make many sacrificies throughout the three years it took to complete this adventure.

The final outcome, this biography of Charles E. McGee, distinguished aviator and American patriot, is possible because of all who assisted. Through their time and effort, Dad's example will reach and inspire a wider circle of people, enriching them as it has those of us fortunate enough to have known and journeyed with him.

Abbreviations

ACSS	Air Command and Staff School	POW	Prisoner of war
ADC	Air Defense Command	ROK	Republic of Korea
AFB	Air Force Base	RON	Remain overnight
AFCS	Air Force Communications Service	ROTC	Reserve Officers Training Corps
AME	African Methodist Episcopal	RSVN	Republic of South Vietnam
APO	Army post office	SAC	Strategic Air Command
BOQ	Bachelor officer's quarters	SOF	Supervisor of flying
BX	Base exchange	TAAF	Tuskegee Army Air Field
CADF	Central Air Defense Force	TAI	Tuskegee Airmen, Incorporated
CCC	Civilian Conservation Corps	TDY	Temporary duty assignment
C.O.	Commanding officer	TRS	TacticalReconnaissance Squadron
D.C.	District of Columbia	U. of I.	University of Illinois
DFC	Distinguished Flying Cross	UN	United Nations
FAA	Federal Aviation Authority	U.S.	United States
FIS	Fighter Interceptor Squadron	USA	United States of America
GI	Government issue	USAEUR	United States Army Europe
K.U.	Kansas University	USAF	United States Air Force
NAACP	National Association for the Advancement of Colored People	USAFE	United States Air Force Europe
NATO	North Atlantic Treaty Organization	USO	United Service Organizations
O.U.	Ohio University	VD	Venereal disease
PCS	Permanent change of station	VIP	Very Important Person
Ph.D.	Doctor of Philosophy	V-J Day	Victory over Japan Day
		WW II	World War II

Prologue

The first time an interviewer asked me who has been influential in my life, I admit I had not given the question much thought. Prior to that, like many children of plenty, there had been no call to examine the sources of my good fortune. Prefacing the query with a comment on the importance of mentors and role models, I think the interviewer expected me to name a significant professor, famous author or civil rights activist, so there appeared to be surprise when I said, "my father."

The idea a father is not readily perceived to be a role model in the black family stands as sad commentary on a blind spot in America, one that overlooks a host of black men leading exemplary lives. Observations aside, when forced to scan the list of possible benefactors, Dad's name came irrepressibly to the top.

"My father, Charles McGee."

The interviewer probed.

"Interesting choice. Why did you pick him?"

"Because, from my earliest memory, he was always encouraging me."

Many things were taught under his watchful eye. Whether to ride a bike down the steepest of hills (or what seemed so when I was six years old) or attend school thousands of miles from home at age thirteen, he instilled in me an early confidence which led me to believe I could meet these and other challenges with some risk taking and hard work.

Looking back, I realize the true value of his wonderful gift. Living in the midst of a racist and sexist society, he could have advocated a cautious path.

"You're a young black girl in a world that doesn't much appreciate you. There are going to be a lot of obstacles. Don't set yourself up for disappointment."

Dad didn't say these words because the thought behind them was foreign to him. Instead, he made me his namesake and endowed me with the sense of purpose and determination that directed his life. It is with gratitude and abiding love, I put his story on paper.

Many significant events, even historic ones, are not recognized at the onset. It may take a series of insights which accumulate over time to finally afford a clear understanding. The legend of men who became Tuskegee Airmen is an example. Dad's story is closely entwined with theirs and it is fitting that my first real appreciation of his indomitable spirit came through them. It happened at the Tuskegee Airmen Convention in Washington, D.C., in August of 1989. My brother, Ronald Allen McGee, and sister, Yvonne Gay McGee, had been attending Tuskegee Airmen, Inc. (TAI) conventions for some time, but it was my introduction. Even though I had known some of Dad's fellow officers since childhood, this was my first close encounter with them in a long time.

I entered the reception hall to be greeted by a sea of silver-haired men of various shades of brown from "light, bright, almost white" to the deepest ebony hue. Most were wearing colored blazers, red, blue, orange and navy among others, creating a kaleidoscope as they clustered in some places and intermingled in others. I learned that the color of the jackets denoted the chapter from which the members hailed. Dad looked very sharp, sporting the sky blue of Kansas City's Heart of America Chapter. A number of Airmen approached us.

"Hey, Mac. Good to see you."

"Colonel, you look great. What's new?"

The greetings flew fast and free along with good-natured glad handing and backslapping. Smiles were broad and genuine and the hand shakes strong and sure.

As the evening progressed, long-standing friendships were acknowledged and renewed. There was the periodic talk of illness and loss that might be expected from men in their sixth and seventh decades, but thoughts of advancing years and frail health paled in comparison to the strength and vitality filling the room that night.

Drinks were ordered and glasses clinked as the Tuskegee Airmen swapped stories old and new. The discussions were punctuated by raucous laughter and interrupted by greetings with each new arrival. It didn't take long to realize the special bond between these men, one I felt privileged to observe. Their strong allegiance was unforgettably compelling and at the same time almost intimidating. The Airmen were gallant and gracious to family and friends, but in the midst of so much camaraderie we were set apart. It was clear we weren't one of "them" and to be one of "them" was clearly very special.

That evening, for one moment I was back in time, witnessing a World War II flight ready room filled with a cadre of top notch fighter pilots. With confident swagger, they exuded fiery, irrepressible energy which left no doubt they were equal to the challenge ahead. These men fought racism at home to reach the battlefront. They worked long and hard to become masters of their fate as they faced war. They shared a common conviction that what they were doing would make a difference beyond the war.

Coming back to the present and the convention hall, it was hard to tell forty-five years had elapsed and for all practical purposes nothing had changed. These men conversed with the same enthusiasm and passion that told everyone they could still do phenomenal things. The Tuskegee Airmen were mortal men with uncommon determination to be more than was expected of them. That night I looked into the familiar face of my father and saw this amazing feature for the first time.

In the years which have passed since the initial insight, I have come to learn much more about the Tuskegee Airmen, gallant aviators, patriots and the first United States African American pilots and crews to serve their country during World War II and to this day. Too often African American men are not portrayed in mainstream America as loving husband, fathers, patriots or role models. In order to dispel ill-conceived notions and share a greater understanding, I commit my father's biography to paper.

This book is drawn from his reflections as he relayed them over the years and in interviews. As narrator of his story, I share observations which are, in great part, the consequences of having him in my life. It is a journey across a century of trial and achievement. It is one for the record.

I: Foundation

1919-1939

- The 1919 Treaty of Versailles ending World War I put heavy demands on Germany, sowing the seeds for future conflict.
- Alcock and Brown completed the first nonstop transatlantic flight in 1919.
- After training in France, Bessie Coleman became the first licensed black pilot in the USA in 1922.
- Following the crash of the New York Stock Market, blacks were hit hard in the Great Depression of the 1930s.
- African Americans helped elect President Franklin D. Roosevelt, who stimulated the economy with the "New Deal" and, with wife Eleanor, was a supporter of civil rights.
- Blacks were admitted into the Civil Pilot Training Program at six black colleges and two non-academic flying schools in 1939.
- Hitler's invasion of Poland signaled the beginning World War II.

None of us influence the circumstances of our birth, and so it was with my father, Charles Edward McGee, born on December 7, 1919 to Lewis Allen McGee and Ruth Elizabeth Lewis McGee. Lewis was a battle tested World War I veteran returned from Europe where he had served as a 1st lieutenant and chaplain for the troops. At the time of Charles' birth the family lived at 425 E. 158th Street in Cleveland, Ohio, another accident of fate since Lewis' work, sometimes as a teacher, social worker and minister of the AME (African Methodist Episcopal) church, resulted in frequent moves.

Charles' brother, Lewis Allen Jr., was born two years before in Raleigh, North Carolina, and the family had lived in several locales before coming to Cleveland. It turned out the Cleveland stint was long enough to welcome the arrival of Ruth Monzella McGee on May 1, 1921. Sadly, it also served as the last earthly home for the children's mother. Ruth died within weeks of the birth of her daughter and namesake from an infection thought to be pneumonia contracted during her confinement at the hospital following childbirth.

Not much can be revealed about the short life of Charles' mother. Though born a Singleton, she was adopted by the Daniel Lewis Family. They lived in Springfield, Ohio, and Ruth most likely spent the greater part of her life there. Lewis Sr. came to know her while he was attending Wilberforce University in Xenia, Ohio, but did not talk about her to his children after her death. Whether she was a student at Wilberforce, Charles didn't know.

There is much I wanted to find out about my paternal grandmother Ruth and how her family coped after losing her at such a young age. Critical events are thought to be better recalled, unless too traumatic, in which case they can be suppressed. Some people say they remember things that happened at a very young age, but for whatever reason the rules of memory dictate, Dad cannot say much about the first decade of his life. When asked about his mother, he is quiet and gets a distant look in eyes peering back seventy five years.

"I have no personal recall of her," he finally answers.

There are bits and pieces of his early years Charles does remember. He remembers his father relating one story about his time at Wilberforce. He had a job on campus grooming and tending horses for the school's ROTC program headed by Colonel Benjamin O. Davis Sr. (Coincidentally, Davis would go on to become the nation's first black general and his son, B. O. Davis Jr., would follow in his footsteps, ultimately leading the country's first black military pilots into the history books. The thought of these developments was almost inconceivable at the time.)

Lewis Sr. also related stories about being the second eldest of three sons and three daughters of Charles Allen and Gay Ankrum McGee, and growing up in a religious home. Charles Allen had been a slave until the age of six. In adult years, he became a Methodist minister, providing a strong spiritual foundation, and with wife Gay offered guidance and encouragement to their growing children. Gay's father, Charles Ankrum, was also an AME minister and a veteran of the Civil War.

Like most Negroes in this country, Gay and her husband Charles had mixed ancestry; hers was of Caucasian, Indian and African roots and his father was Scottish, but whether he was a slave owner or abolitionist is not known. Mixing of the races persisted despite anti-miscegenation laws against marriage or sexual relations between a man and woman of different races, especially between a white and a black.

Multiracial heritage prompted laws which defined racial identity in cases like the McGee's. Just as brown eyes are dominant over blue eyes genetically, black lineage dominated. One thirty-second of black ancestry in the blood line, which equates to black parentage six generations passed, qualified a man or woman as Negro in most states with laws addressing racial identity.

Lewis Sr. was a prominent and handsome man. He was close to six feet tall and fair-skinned with dark wavy hair. While it might not have been apparent to the casual observer that Lewis was a Negro, he was never known to misrepresent his heritage. His wife Ruth had been brown skinned, quiet and unassumingly attractive in her own right. Their children spanned the colors between with Lewis Jr. being the darkest, Ruth very pale and Charles a honey color in the middle.

In the summer of 1921, Lewis Sr. was 27 years old and a widower faced with the prospects of rearing three small children alone. It is hard to imagine how their world must have viewed this motherless rainbow family. Though details of life in Cleveland remains behind the veil of lost childhood memories, periodic visits with Lewis' mother in Clarksburg and Morgantown, West Virginia, emerge in snatches. Lewis Jr., Charles and Ruth were put on a train in Cleveland and the conductor kept an eye on them until they were delivered into the hands of relatives waiting on the other end. The great "iron" steps onto the train looked pretty formidable to a little guy and while all of this was strange to Charles at first, he soon adjusted to the new adventure. When the time was right, the conductor let them eat the packed lunch, which was sent with them. For the rest of the trip they amused themselves as children are prone to do and the time passed quickly.

In Morgantown there was a boardwalk leading up to the house. Lewis Jr., Charles and Ruth played on it and school yard swings where Charles first soared high to momentarily escape the bonds of earth's gravity. The time was not right, however, and one flight ended abruptly in a painful fall to the blacktop. Charles announced his distress for the entire world to hear as he ran to the house where Grandma Gay cleaned his wounded chin and dried his tears.

During those summer visits with Grandma Gay, she created a special place for them, one nurturing and comforting and filled with the love a departed mother could not offer. For that, I am grateful.

"Thank you, Mama Gay."

Patched up, Charles headed back to the swing set and unfinished business. The safer swing on the porch and the front step offered the best vantage point for family to gather to observe the end of the summer day. There they would relive times gone by, talk of hopes for tomorrow and watch events unfolding before them. During the evening and into the night, the aroma of fresh bread from the bakery nearby floated down the hillside and wafted through the valley.

Of course, things were not always so serene. Kids being kids, Lewis, Charles and Ruth got into their share of mischief. Charles took a turn throwing mud balls at freshly laundered sheets flapping on the clothesline, although he denied involvement in the prank. With both father and grandfathers being ministers, it is not surprising that playing church in the backyard was another favorite pastime. Mama Gay laughed at Charles' portrayal of the minister and, especially, the ending of his sermons. According to her version of the story, he was overheard delivering this closing line.

"Now it's time to sing one more song and get out of here."

"They tell me the story," Charles said, "but I don't remember anything like that either."

Sometimes the visits to West Virginia took place during the winter. An iron cook stove in the kitchen had to be stoked with wood. Helping fetch wood was the perfect job for a youngster underfoot. Often a treat was the reward and gingerbread was Charles' favorite. (To this day he still gets pleasure from the first bite of hot gingerbread cut from the corner of the baking tin.)

When Charles was eight years old, his father's work took the family south for a year, where Lewis completed a teaching assignment at Edward Waters College in Jacksonville, Florida. While it wasn't common for a Negro to have a higher education in 1927, Lewis was a graduate of Wilberforce College in Ohio, an accomplishment qualifying him for the appointment.

Lewis Sr. moved the children into a little cabin near the edge of town next to a sugar cane field. Cane fields were a place to play after school and the sweet taste of fresh cut cane was an added bonus. Crabs cooking in a tub over a backyard fire left indelible memories, as did Lewis Jr. being kicked by a mule he had the misfortune of following too closely.

Another recollection related to school and was not so pleasant. The Florida schools for Negroes hadn't kept pace with their northern counterparts and as a result, Charles had to repeat the third grade when the family returned to Cleveland.

In 1929, the stock market crashed, beginning economic chaos in America. Back in Cleveland, Lewis continued to be mother and father to children now eleven, nine and seven. Even in the best of circumstances they must have been quite a handful, but now resources were extremely meager and times difficult. Late in the year, Lewis moved on to Chicago, following job opportunities in social work.

Rather than keeping the children with him in the unstable situation they faced, he arranged for them to stay with Hershall and Harriet Harris, who were affectionately called Mom and Pop Harris. They lived in St. Charles, Illinois, about forty miles west of Chicago on the Fox River. By reputation and deed, the Harris' were good people. Over the years, they had raised a number of children whose parents had been unable to care for them for one reason or another. Hershall worked in a foundry at the edge of town and although there were very few blacks in the area, the Harris' were long time residents of the community.

Unlike Chicago, St. Charles was a small town providing a safe haven where the children were able to grow and thrive under the watchful eye of the close-knit Harris family. Mrs. Harris' brother, William Luckett, who was a commercial artist, lived next door. He had a croquet court and thriving apple tree in the yard between their homes. The children had freedom to explore the woods and roam fields for hours at a time, and they took advantage of it, within the bounds set by the Harris'. These bounds imposed real limitations since the Harris' were known for their strict code of conduct, a reputation which survived into my day.

In addition to their homework, Charles and the other children had regular chores, including mopping the kitchen floor, raking the yard and clearing fallen apples, and keeping their bedrooms straight. Children were to conduct themselves appropriately and know how to address their elders. Good manners were central to good living and "yes ma'ms" and "no sirs" were expected. There was a price to pay for infractions and "spare the rod and spoil the child" was more than just a motto for foster children as well as natural born Harris'.

Charles' years in St. Charles spanned third grade through the first year of high school. Because there were so few blacks, the schools were integrated and Charles became more aware of ethnic differences. Walking or riding a bike was the main form of transportation and passing through neighborhoods delivering newspapers gave him the opportunity to learn their distinct make up. Some near the foundry were Polish or of another European extraction. There was name calling occasionally.

"Usually young folks' mischief," he explained, "but like they say, words don't hurt you."

The St. Charles years passed intermingling strict rules with climbing mulberry trees, riding bikes along the edge of town, skipping stones from the riverbank, and a notable trip to the World's Fair in Chicago. Lewis and Charles joined the Boy Scouts of America where patriotic values of loyalty, bravery and service, consistent with their Christian upbringing, were strengthened. The quest for personal challenge carried Charles to the ranks of Eagle Scout. From scouting experiences he gained an enduring sense of the importance of brotherhood and service to others before self.

In years to come, Dad would take his family back to this boyhood home to visit the Harris'. On the ride there he told us how they helped raise him and his sister and brother. It was clear he developed a great affection for them, even as he cautioned us to mind our manners before we got out of the car. To this day I remember the story of Ma Harris smacking a girl "silly" for putting red polish on her toenails after being told not to. I questioned the harsh treatment.

"She should have done what she was told," my father replied.

If not before, the healthy respect for discipline which served Charles throughout life was nurtured during his years in St. Charles.

During Charles' sophomore year in high school, his father accepted an AME church assignment and moved his children to Keokuk, Iowa. In 1935, The Great Depression was in full force, but the era was not much different from any other for folks who never had much.

"Life was meager all through these years, whether we're talking Ohio, Illinois or Iowa. In Cleveland we always had food, but not a lot of clothes. What we had was always clean and had patches on it put there by Mama Gay, Mrs. Harris or whoever. We didn't have a lot, never had a lot, but were aware that whatever we had was enough."

To a certain extent poverty, like beauty, is in the eyes of the beholder.

"We each had a change of clothes...and shoes. I remember putting newspaper in my shoes when I wore a hole in the leather so my feet wouldn't get cold so quickly in the winter time."

It wasn't something that made Charles feel he was on the low end of the social or economic strata. It was just the nature of the times because there was the depression and everybody was suffering along. He knew there were some people who were better off. They had big houses with tennis courts and lived in another part of town, but that wasn't something the McGee family dwelled on.

Neither was racism. Reverend McGee had high ideals and believed in a vision of a world in which people treated each other equally, as brothers and sisters in the sight of God. Not only did he live by this principle, he also passed it on. So, Lewis Jr., Charles and Ruth learned to treat others as they wished to be treated. Ideals set the tone.

It is tempting to believe that being black is the single most defining attribute for a young child in America. What children are led to believe, and more importantly, come to accept about their circumstances, including race and ethnicity, ultimately defines their future.

The reality was most day to day living for Negro youngsters took place separate and apart from mainstream white America. Racial strife was remote for children living among their own people in a closed society. Overhearing comments by adults, they began to conceive of the outside world, but their real frame of reference was closer to home.

That's not to say Charles and other black children were protected from ridicule in their own backyard. Children of all persuasions grasp differences and use them as weapons to gain advantage. Exploitation of differences (height, weight, clothing, accent, background and so forth) is something most people have experienced. Growing up in the black community, being very dark or very light dramatically increases the likelihood of being singled out, teased and in the worst case ostracized. Charles being light-skinned and no exception was tested at a young age.

In Keokuk the picture began to change. He lived in two worlds, going to a predominantly white high school and living on the "colored" east side of town near his Dad's AME church.

Charles was a good student, prior admonitions and strict regimens already paying dividends. He was active in the school chorus and sports, although an early injury permanently ended his football days. Following an ill-fated tackle, he lay on the bottom of the pile and realized something was wrong. When he tried to stand up, pain made the injury obvious. His collar bone was broken. For weeks one arm was bound to his chest while the fracture mended and when healed a knot remained at the site of the break as a permanent reminder.

Basketball became his sport of choice after the football injury. Charles' love for music also blossomed during high school years. The French horn intrigued him and orchestral music was thrilling. He would have loved to play in the band, but the cost of an instrument was beyond his means. His voice on the other hand was free. He chose to participate in school chorus, an affinity increased by attraction to a lovely dark skinned girl who was also a member. Charles walked her home once, but as fortune and the girl's parents would have it, their relationship was short-lived.

"On occasion, I wonder what happened to her, " Charles acknowledged wistfully, a strain of music echoing from the past.

According to Charles, dating was different in the 1930s. There was little one on one or even double dating in his crowd. Young people usually did things in groups. A boy and girl may have an eye on each other. The two may even exchange a Christmas card or present. Virginia Tolliver was Charles first real date, a walk home from school. He liked her a lot. She liked him too, but her folks thought her too young for such "goings on." Although their lives went separate ways, Charles never forgot her.

On hot summer days everyone, white and black, would go to the park for an outing. Blankets would be spread under a big shade tree. People enjoyed jumping into the muddy Mississippi River to cool off on a lazy afternoon.

"If you put your feet down you could feel all the muck, so you'd just jump in the water and start swimming. There wasn't much standing around."

The process of understanding how his race made his life different was under way by high school. Charles' early education, with few exceptions, took place in predominantly white schools. The number of blacks in St. Charles and Keokuk was so small, all youngsters attended the same school. It was not a conscious attempt to integrate the races; it just wasn't economically feasible to segregate them. Prejudice manifested itself in both overt and subtle ways, neither of which escaped his attention nor that of the other black students.

"Oh sure there was racism," Charles observed without rancor. "There was prejudice in the town, because the town had a theater and you (Negroes) had to sit in the balcony."

About name calling, "Sometimes I'd be called nigger boy by kids on the street."

There were white students who befriended him only to be advised against it by less tolerant classmates. There was the inevitable caution.

"You don't need to get so buddy buddy with him."

Afterwards, no more invitations would be extended to join in after school games or outings.

Closing of ranks when the wall of segregation was breached was not an isolated phenomenon. Social interaction could be a precursor to intimacy and, therefore, threatened carefully erected barriers and raised anxieties. "Well meaning" proponents of social order often interceded to keep things from going too far for the "good of all."

In reality these were patronizing acts of racism. Lessons passed down for generations in the McGee family dictated Charles endure them with quiet dignity. So he turned a deaf ear and kept his feelings to himself. By not confronting their racist attitudes, he showed the boys more respect and common regard than they afforded him. Each incident shaped his consciousness and set the stage for future encounters in which he would not be acquiescent.

In many ways, it was easier for Charles to disregard the more blatant verbal assaults and social snubs than the racial biases in the educational system itself. Despite his outstanding performances, there were occasions when Charles did not get the recognition due him. Whether it was getting second place in the speech contest or the citizenship award he didn't win, the bias was sometimes so obvious that even white kids commented.

"You should have gotten first place. Probably the only reason you didn't is because you're Negro."

Other times it would be the solo part not considered appropriate for a colored student.

"In those days, good hearted whites would try to find a part that might be more 'typical,' so black students could participate in this type of thing (plays or chorus)."

Charles was more troubled by displays of unfairness in school. Any discrimination is disturbing, but name calling by a stranger on the street can be more easily dismissed as ignorance.

"Sticks and stones may break my bones, but words can never hurt me."

Education was supposed to be the path to a better life. Charles' betrayal in the very institution he had been taught to revere was a particularly bitter pill. In swallowing it, it is understandable he too could become bitter and resentful. Charles, however, would not.

Perhaps his resilience stemmed from the affirmation he received from Mama Gay, the discipline instilled by the Harris' or his father's religious teachings that all God's children are created in his image and equally important. Maybe it was his own inner voice that wouldn't make room for self doubt, but some how he was able to put these racist experiences into a larger perspective. Rather than destructive forces, they became building blocks developing his strength of character. A chip on his shoulder would not advance his cause.

Two years later in 1937, he returned to Chicago.

Charles' last year in high school was a solitary time. After years of being widowed, Lewis Sr. had taken a second wife, Luvinia, who like Lewis was involved in social work. The introduction of Luvinia came as quite a surprise, if not to the family who lived so long without a mother in the home, to me and my brother and sister who had never known of a second (actually first) step grandmother. Dad, always the gentleman, was uncharacteristically vague about her short tenure and ultimate fate.

"I don't know what actually happened to her," he reflected. "Her life style was not very compatible with that (expected) of a minister's wife."

Obviously, she did not share some of the McGee values.

I probed to learn more about this newly introduced, albeit short-lived, member of the family.

"Well, as I recall, she did like to drink after a day's work. She started on a bottle of beer.... I just know when Dad left Chicago and went to Gary, she didn't go. We lived on Michigan Avenue near 55th Street (Garfield Boulevard and Michigan) not far from Dusable High School. She had her room (in the apartment) and some evenings I would see her. Dad was back and forth (between Gary and Chicago), but not around enough for me to know exactly what was happening.... They didn't divorce at that time, but it was obvious it was not going to work. I was really kind of on my own, fighting the battle to do well and stay in school."

Enough said.

Lewis Jr. was away at Wheaton College. His experience there was the beginning of an estrangement from the family. It became apparent in following years that dogmatic religious beliefs Lewis Jr. was exposed to at school would irrevocably change the close relationship he and Charles had enjoyed.

Around the same time the decision was made for Ruth to attend Englewood, a girl's school in West Virginia. Without a female role model in the home, a controlled environment was thought best for a teenage girl. With Lewis Sr. in Gary, Charles, now eighteen years old, was for the most part left to fend for himself. Returning to Chicago, Charles' previous academic misfortunes were reversed, because this time his new school was behind the one in Iowa.

"I didn't have to do anything for six weeks because of the difference."

With numerous temptations, the urban playground presented Charles with important choices in his young life. The street scene was alluring and a youthful lust for life drew many young men to wine, women, and the pursuit of pleasure, particularly in the absence of a strong guiding parent in the home. The course he chose to follow had been carefully laid in his formative years and he was not inclined to deviate or indulge in the excesses of the day. He would not be distracted. Instead, he applied himself to his studies and set his sight on a college education, which he had been taught was the key to a successful future.

"All along folks kept asking what I was taking in high school. In other words, enter the college preparatory route. The difference was a lot more English, math and science. I just knew that you had to get to college."

About his social life in those days, Charles stifled a laugh. Obviously the frame of reference was very different for a teenager in the thirties versus the sixties. Patiently, he explained without specifically saying, the idea of having a social life required money. In the absence of one, you don't consider the other. What little socializing there was took place around school, chorus and glee club or church activities. Charles took odd jobs like washing and starching walls (to keep them clean) at Provident Hospital and sometimes used the money he earned to go to the movies, a rare treat.

"There was one girl I liked. She graduated in the same class. Her parents didn't want her seeing anybody 'lighter' than her. Then there was another lady I made contact with, a classmate who went to the theater with me. When I left for college, we kept in touch a time or two before losing contact. I can't remember her name. Sometimes it comes back. Oh yes, her name was Emelda Charles, the only girl in her family for a couple generations."

Knowing that cooking was never one of Dad's fortes, I was curious about how he managed meals on his own. Scrambled eggs, a specialty of his, were most likely on the menu but what else? Members of the fast food generations will be appalled to know that a can of beans or soup often sufficed for a meal or late night snack.

Charles spent the year before he graduated from DuSable High School in the spring of 1938 in a spartan fashion. He made use of his time studying and as a result graduated ninth in a class of four hundred and thirty-six students. After high school, Charles planned to work for a year to make money for college. Luvinia, through connections she had, was able to get him a job with the Civilian Conservation Corps (CCC). In late 1938 and early 1939, Charles worked on various road and farm projects with 2664 Company in Mt. Carroll in northern Illinois and saved his money. The Corps was almost like a military camp. You got a uniform and a paycheck while you learned a skill and served the country. In Mt. Carroll, Charles worked with engineers, handling the transit and laying out contours. During that time he developed an interest in civil engineering which followed him into college.

While Charles was hard at work with Roosevelt's CCC Program, a bitter Adolph Hitler was leading the Nazi Party on a steady course of revenge for the harsh treatment Germans encountered after losing World War I. By September of that year, Hitler had taken control of Czechoslovakia, and with the help of Joseph Stalin, the Germans and Russians captured Poland. Polish Jews were being exterminated. Britain declared war on Germany and began sending troops into France. Hitler had his eyes on Norway to secure a foothold from which to launch an attack against Britain.

Rumblings of the war going on in Europe were starting to be heard in the U.S., but Charles and other young men his age were vaguely aware of them. For the most part, they were more absorbed with recovering from the depression and getting on with life in this country. The trouble abroad was too distant to have any real bearing on a young black man working to get into college.

"Even though things were building up in late '39, there was no emphasis on the war until later when the draft started in 1940."

Charles' thoughts had not yet turned skyward to imagine adventures there. Though they would become his heroes, he was unaware of Bessie Coleman's determination to fly, which led her to France when no flying school in this country would admit a black woman, and Charles Alfred Anderson's record as the first black to complete a transcontinental flight. He did not know of unprecedented advances made in aviation in the 1930s or that 125 black Americans held pilot licenses in 1939. In fact, nothing in his childhood or early experiences foretold what was to come. No memories of crop dusters over the sugar cane fields or stunt fliers in newsreels at the cinema. As he packed up his few belongings, took his savings and headed for Champaign-Urbana and his first year at the University of Illinois, his greatest passions in life had not yet been revealed.

II: College Years

1940-1942
- In 1940, Congress passed a law requiring all males between 21 and 35 to register for military service.
- President Roosevelt issued Executive Order 8802 banning discrimination in companies doing business with the government and formed the Fair Employment Practice Committee.
- Against the wishes of the War Department, the U.S. Congress, bowing to pressure from Negro leaders and media, activated the first all-black Fighter Squadron at Tuskegee Institute, Alabama.
- On December 7, 1941, Pearl Harbor was bombed and the United States declared war on Japan.
- Allied forces fought Italian and German forces in Northern Africa in 1942.

Black students at the University of Illinois in 1940 were few and far between. There was no housing for them on campus so most, not being locals, had to find rooms in Champaign's North End, home to the majority of the Negro population. Charles took up residence with the Brown family who lived on the corner of 6th and White Street. At first, his "room" was in the basement in a finished space by the furnace, but soon after he moved up to the second floor room with an outside entrance added to accommodate a boarder. He had a place to stay, along with his own shelf in the Browns' ice box: the basic necessities, once he provided the food.

A new engineering student on campus, he soon was introduced to a small group of fellow classmates in similar circumstances, who left the black neighborhood to cross town to the white university, a trek that set them apart from most who lived in the North End. Bonds developed as they shared universal college experiences, from study and intellectual debates to social activities and romance.

Though Charles' head was deep in the books, Frances Edwina Nelson was able to turn it. He never forgot the first time he saw her. She was among friends who had gathered on the college green known as the Quad. A tall, brown-skinned beauty with long legs, long hair and penetrating dark eyes, she made quite an impression.

To his great disappointment, those unforgettable eyes did not look his direction and he didn't even manage an introduction.

The next time Charles saw Frances was following Sunday school services several weeks later. Shortly after coming to Champaign, Charles had joined Bethel AME Church continuing to practice his family's African Methodist faith. Frances and her immediate family were members of Salem Baptist Church which was one block east of Bethel. In time honored tradition, young people would gather after services in the block between these prominent pillars of the black community. A weekly ritual, the purpose was to see and be seen before parents whisked their sons and daughters away. On one of these occasions, Charles maneuvered his way over and managed an introduction to Frances, but by her account she did not find the meeting memorable. She was enamored with another young man, Welton "Ike" Taylor, who with her held the campus title for king and queen of jitterbug.

"She had her eye on Ike, so she didn't remember our first meeting."

Frances' family had standing in the Champaign-Urbana community. Her father, Franklin Joseph Nelson, had been a successful businessman and land owner, who left his widow Nellie Carter Nelson (Momma Nellie) and their two children, Leonard and Frances, well provided for after his death in 1935.

Among the land holdings he left his heirs was the large family home at 607 N. Hickory Street, which still had the attached general store Franklin operated for decades. The home served as a boarding house for permanent residents as well as transient visitors. Charles learned Frances was living at home while attending the University. Focusing on the business of being a student, he stayed in the background and waited for her jitterbug partner to fade from the scene.

Living in a relatively small and close knit community had its advantages. Before long their paths crossed again. Not all the Nelsons were Baptists. Frances had a older half brother, Cecil, who was born to Franklin and his first wife. Cecil Nelson and wife Carrie were members of Bethel AME, a circumstance which worked in Charles' favor when they invited Momma Nellie to attend a Sunday afternoon program and she brought Frances along. During the program, a Tom Thumb wedding was planned for the following Sunday afternoon. By a stroke of fate, Charles and Frances were chosen to play the bride and groom. Charles allowed himself the luxury of imagining he was the reason she agreed to participate. At that affair they became acquainted.

No one suspected the Tom Thumb Wedding was a harbinger of things to come.

Life at the U. of I. was a great adventure for Charles his first semester. The discipline that got him through high school was being challenged on a new level. It was a time to apply himself to his studies. No matter what lay ahead, Charles knew education was the path to personal growth and scholarly pursuits the key to professional success.

Another goal of his was to be a member of the Alpha Phi Alpha fraternity and to do that he had to make good grades. The fact his dad and uncle were Alphas may have influenced him, but beyond that, Charles liked the things the fraternity stood for. The fraternity motto summarized it: "First of all, servants of all, we shall transcend all."

The "Big Brothers" on campus were a principled, studious bunch which also appealed to Charles. Some members like Dunbar McLaurin were graduate students, a rare occurrence for young black men of the era. The Alphas had a house near the campus which was another attraction. Living there would eliminate the long walk from the North End. Charles along with six other Alpha aspirants joined the line of pledges.

The road to brotherhood had its obstacles. They were set intentionally to test the mettle of Sphinxmen, the name given to Alpha pledges. Entry was the objective, pledging was the pathway, and hazing was the norm. No matter how smart and savvy Sphinxmen were in other settings, when "Big Brother" was around, there was no questioning his authority.

The inferior status of pledges subjected them to various demands they had to carry out on the spot.

"Recite *Invictus*."

"Recite *If*."

Being prepared to perform more "erudite" orders was essential, but not all commands were so scholarly.

"Count all the bricks in the north wall of Huff Gym!"

"Yes, Big Brother! No, Big Brother! And no excuse, Big Brother!" were replies expected from the pledges.

"Drop and give me twenty (push ups)" and "assume the position" (paddles were not merely ornamental) were frequent commands from the already inducted Alpha Men.

All and all, the hazing by Tau Chapter was not as vicious or extreme as some Greek organizations. The pledging was more directed toward discipline, bonding, and ultimately loyalty among brothers. The common objective was worthy. (Ironically, aspects of pledging were not unlike military training imposed for many of the same reasons.)

By second semester, Charles had ended his days as a pledge. He passed the tests, made the grades and "crossed the burning sands," becoming an Alpha Man.

Charles knew Frances loved to dance and despite the strict rules laid down by Momma Nellie, she managed to stop by the Kappa Alpha Psi House to indulge this passion as often as possible. Unlike the Alphas, the Kappas were known for their open parties and Charles envied them for no other reason than her visits. At the Kappa House, Frances was a regular in the "enter at your own risk" room reserved for the most daring and accomplished jitterbugs. Not in her league on the dance floor, he watched, stepped in on slow dances and bided his time.

When the draft started in 1940, Charles received his draft card from Gary, Indiana. At the time, college students weren't being called.

"I always remember I had a bicycle at Dad's place in Gary and I don't remember the number...might have been something like 1709, but the license of my bicycle and the draft card number were exactly the same."

He was struck by the coincidence.

Charles, working hard as an engineering major, was also enrolled in ROTC and a member of Pershing Riffles, an elite drill team. Academic rigors coupled with social distractions to take their toll, and second semester Charles' grades began to suffer. At the same time his funds were dwindling. Summer employment was essential for him to have enough cash to return to school the following year. The answer to his financial woes lay in the steel mills of Gary, Indiana.

On July 19,1941, as 21 year old Charles toiled in the mills, thirteen young Negro men gathered on the campus of Tuskegee Institute, Alabama, to form the first class of black pilot trainees for the Army Air Corps.

In the mills of the Carnegie Illinois Steel Company, Charles pulled the graveyard shift on a construction crew. Along with other blacks who were fortunate enough to find employment in the steel industry, his assignments were the menial, back breaking tasks of running concrete for the furnaces or mopping up the foundry buildings, but the pay was more than most other jobs and therefore a necessary means to the desired end.

Occasionally, after a long evening on the job, Charles mustered the energy to go into Chicago to enjoy night life the city offered. The early morning bus ride back and precious few hours of sleep before his next shift were deterrents to keep him from making it a regular habit. When he let his mind wonder, it consistently settled on a young woman enjoying less arduous summer days in Champaign, but his budget permitted no more than daydreams. So he applied himself to work and hoped his absence would not provide an unfair advantage to rivals for Frances' affection. Short term sacrifice for long term gain! It was a principle already ingrained in his philosophy.

The war in Europe would not be fended off by aspirations of higher education or thoughts of budding love. In response to increasing concern about events overseas, the draft was reaching into the sanctuary of the college classroom. In the beginning it was easy to resist the notion he would become involved, especially before finishing school. That was no longer the case.

Not long after returning to campus in 1941, Charles was between classes heading south from Wesley Foundation to the Chemistry Building. He spotted Frances walking toward Green Street. They spoke briefly as their paths crossed. After taking a few steps, Charles turned hoping to get another glimpse of her. To his delight, she had done the same and was looking back too. Their eyes met, she smiled and, in that brief exchange, doubt evaporated and the mystical die was cast.

Afterward, they spent time together at church and Frances consented when he asked to walk her home from classes. From then they were together whenever possible. Without a lot of money, "library dates" were frequent. Charles credited these with getting him back on track academically. He had changed his major to Life Sciences and was making the Dean's List. Nevertheless, it was a struggle to stay in school. Tuition and housing were a big expenses and after they were taken care of he was lucky to have a nickel to buy an apple. To earn money for food, he bussed dishes at one of the fraternity houses and the Champaign Country Club.

By the end of the semester just about everyone knew of someone who had been drafted. Charles' father had served as a commissioned officer and chaplain with the infantry in France during World War I. He spoke enough about his experience to paint a vivid picture of life as a ground soldier in combat and it was grim. Yet what option did Charles have? If called upon, he knew he would have to slosh through muddy woods and fields and endure bitter cold while living in uncomfortable encampments and fighting from foxholes. The thought was more than a little unsettling. Though he began to wonder, he didn't know what other choice he had.

On December 7, 1941 Charles was visiting his father and anticipating a quiet 22nd birthday. At 4:00 pm, while riding with members of the Coleridge Taylor Glee Club from Gary to a church in South Chicago for an evening vespers program, he heard numbing news coming across the radio.

"Today at 7:50 am, Pacific time, the Japanese bombed Pearl Harbor...."

The United States declared war against Japan. While the glee club went on with the show that night, the year ahead was suddenly filled with uncertainty and Charles knew that one way or another, we were going to be involved in war.

Back together on campus, he and Frances knew his call to service was just a matter of time. Each day was precious and tomorrow offered no promises, only the hope of being together. They started going steady. Day by day, life went on and Charles continued school and work. In the meantime, Lewis Sr., Lewis Jr. and Ruth, responding to the build up of armed forces, volunteered for the military service.

Early in 1942, as Charles contemplated his fate, news of a possible alternative began to circulate around campus. According to the grapevine, colored soldiers would be taught to fly at

Chanute Field in Rantoul, Illinois, just north of Champaign. (As it turned out, non-flying support personnel in communications, engineering, armament and mechanics were being trained at Chanute Field and pilot training was at a remote training school near Tuskegee, Alabama. There, the wife of the President of the United States, Eleanor Roosevelt, had flown with a black pilot, Charles Alfred "Chief" Anderson of the Civilian Pilot Training Program. She was visiting Tuskegee Institute to look into research being done on infantile paralysis, her husband's illness. To the shock of her secret service agents, the flight with "Chief" was an impromptu decision she made. The highly publicized event helped counter skepticism about the ability of blacks to fly and changed lives and history. Mrs. Roosevelt subsequently was reported to have told her husband that if the country was going to train pilots for the coming war, some of them ought to be black.)

The rumored program was real. The War Department approved Army Air Corps plans for an all-black pursuit squadron and funds for training enlisted support personnel at the Air Corps Technical School at Chanute Field in January of 1941. Primary pilot training was awarded to Tuskegee Institute with more advanced instruction slated for Tuskegee Army Air Field to be constructed nearby. From its inception, there had been attempts to scuttle the program, but the war effort needed more pilots and despite racist attitudes, no more impediments to stall the trial program could be justified. The first all-black class (42C, following the Corps wide convention of naming the 3rd class in each training program in 1942) was in training and Tuskegee Army Air Field was preparing for more trainees. On March 6, 1942, five black men completed the program, four taking the oath of office and pinning on the wings that told the world they were pilots. The fifth graduate, Captain B. O. Davis Jr., commissioned at West Point in 1936, had at last accomplished his long cherished wish to become a pilot.

Closer to home there was tangible evidence of the program's existence. Fifteen miles north of Champaign at Chanute Field, Colored non flying personnel were being trained to support the 99th Pursuit pilots in Tuskegee. Frances' nephews, Ernest and Cecil Jr., entered the Chanute program. True enough, a quiet recruiting campaign had been launched to find a select number of candidates to undergo the tough screening process. Those gaining admission entered the strenuous training designed to transform them into a combat unit in the Army Air Corp.

Charles decided to apply. In April of 1942, he was sent to northern Indiana to take the written and physical exams. The screening was unique to Charles and having a black applicant was apparently unique to the recruitment officers, as well.

"There was a guy there who had never dealt with any blacks and he kept filling in the blanks wrong because he was writing (I was) white."

Charles wanted to fly. The decision was not hard. Even with the application submitted, the road to Tuskegee proved to be formidable. The next big hurdle was escaping the long arm of the draft. It took months for applications to move through channels and while the draft could be manipulated for a well-connected few, it was a good bet no favors were granted the ordinary man. Like so many institutions, the draft was political, and it was highly unlikely for a poor black boy to pull strings necessary to delay his call, especially while awaiting orders to a little known "Tuskegee Experiment." In fact, during the anxious months of hoping and waiting to hear their fate, several aspirants were drafted and had to board the troop trains and report to boot camp.

Some of these draftees pleaded for consideration.

"I've applied for air training. What can be done?"

The response was, "Well, you're in the infantry now, boy."

Few who were drafted transferred to flying.

In late spring of '42, Charles learned he had passed the test and was accepted in the program. Now it was a question of which call to duty would come first.

After the semester he went back to the mills, but unlike the preceding summer, he spent hard earned money to make the trip to Champaign whenever he could. Mrs. Foster, one of Momma Nellie's boarders, frequently sat on the screened front porch and often was the first to announce his arrival.

"Frances, that 'ole square headed boy is here to see you."

The affection they all felt toward Charles was not veiled by the teasing and banter exchanged.

On those visits, he walked downtown with Frances and her mother, carrying the sacks from their shopping excursions. There were evening strolls hand in hand at the county fair. Long talks began to guardedly explore plans for their future after the war.

On those summer evenings Charles and Frances sat on the porch of the house on Hickory Street. They escaped there to have some time alone, for it was hard to make even the most innocent contact under Momma Nellie's watchful eye.

In addition to a kiss, on one night Charles gave his love an engagement ring. With her consent to marry him, they embarked on a lifelong adventure. The night of their engagement was no exception to the vigil kept by Nellie. Shortly after ten o'clock, the lights on the porch flashed, signaling their fleeting time together was ending.

Charles' future was tied to the draft. As it happened he was never called. A member of Lewis Sr.'s AME church who was also a member of the local draft board knew of his acceptance to the Tuskegee flight school. Charles didn't know it at the time, but this benefactor arranged for his position in the lottery to be "suspended" until he received his orders to report to the special program.

"Years later, on a visit back to Gary, she told me she would just slide my card out of the bunch so they'd pass over it until I got called."

Returning to school in September, 1942, Frances and Charles faced two big decisions. Frances had graduated cum laude from U. of I. and worked for a professor; Charles had two more years. Considering the options, they agreed he would not enroll for the semester as money was hard to come by to be spent on a semester which in all probability would not be completed. In the face of so much uncertainty, the two knew the main thing they wanted was to spend whatever time they had together.

"We had to make another decision. If I was drafted or called up to Tuskegee where would that leave us? We finally decided to get married."

They set the date, completed hurried arrangements while Charles worked on in the mills, and married on Saturday, October 17. Lewis Sr. came to officiate at his son's wedding. The ceremony took place in Frances' Hickory Street home which had been gaily decorated for the occasion with fall foliage. Momma Nellie and Grandmother Gay were present. A fraternity brother, Nathaniel "Nate" Green, from Chicago served as best man. Stella, Frances' sister-in-law, was the matron of honor. Frances' brother Leonard, like Lewis Jr. and Cecil, was already in the service and unable to attend.

The traditional honeymoon was not in their plans. The morning after the wedding, Charles and Frances headed to Gary to begin their life together. Living with a friend, they had a room to themselves and the bonus, a shelf in the ice box.

I imagine it could not have seemed closer to perfect.

Forgetting the mounting turmoil around them, their world was fresh and new and ever so briefly, time stood still.

On Monday, October 19, 1942, the mail brought Charles' orders. On October 26, he was sworn into the enlisted reserves in preparation for entering Army Air Corps aviation cadet training.

III: The Tuskegee Experience

1942-1943

- The first successful nuclear chain reaction ushered in the atomic age.
- After numerous delays, the all-black 99th Fighter Squadron left Tuskegee to join the war in Northern Africa in April, 1943.
- Racial violence erupted on the home front in Detroit and Harlem during the summer of 1943.
- The Allies invaded Sicily in July, 1943; Italy surrendered unconditionally in September and in October joined Allied forces against German troops still fighting on Italian soil.
- Allied leaders Roosevelt, Churchill and Stalin held a summit in Tehran, Iran, to plan war strategies.

Charles reported to Tuskegee Air Field Field on November 24, 1942. He and Frances only had a few weeks to pack their belongings, which was more than ample given the few items they had accumulated. The newlyweds had no intentions of being so quickly separated and together they made the trip to Tuskegee, Alabama, 47 miles east of Montgomery. Frances planned to find a job and room close to Tuskegee Air Field, where Charles would be occupied with training six or seven days a week.

In 1942, the trip south was more than a notion for the young black couple accustomed to life north of the Mason-Dixon line. Patterns of discrimination in the North were more subtle, but in the South of the 1940s, rigid Jim Crow laws of segregation were the way of life. The Air Corps had no intention of disrupting these established practices. To the contrary, they were as deeply ingrained in the culture of the Corps as in the wider society.

For cadets making the trip south on troop trains, the transition was immediately apparent. At the last stop in the north, they had to move from their coach seats, occupied at the beginning of the trip, to those directly behind the engine and coal cars. There, recruits contended with cinder filled smoke and fumes from the train's engines and for the remainder of the trip were denied entry to the dining car. Stations along the way prominently displayed "colored" and "white" signs separating drinking fountains and rest rooms. This was standard treatment for black soldiers preparing to fight and willing to make the ultimate sacrifice for their country.

Rolling along the Illinois Central railway, Charles' thoughts were full of the excitement of taking on a new challenge and worry about how he and Frances would be treated in the south. They did not miss the first appearance of "White Only" signs in southern Illinois, directing Negroes who needed food or rest to out of the way locations and substandard facilities. Charles' days in the south in Florida were a faded memory and Frances was sheltered from the cruel realities of racial hatred during childhood visits to Momma Nellie's family in Moss Point, Mississippi. There had not been much to prepare them for Tuskegee, Alabama, but strictly enforced segregation introduced during their travel began to acclimate them even before they arrived.

Tuskegee Army Air Field (TAAF) was in Macon County, Alabama, near the towns of Tuskegee and Tuskegee Institute. The school, founded by Dr. Booker T. Washington in 1881, was a private Negro college with technical and professional emphases and a trades program. Before the "Tuskegee Experiment" was embarked on, the college operated Moton Field airstrip where Negroes could earn a private pilot license. Tuskegee Institute had successfully bid for the primary training phase of the experimental program. (The Tuskegee Experiment was the War Department's name for the program to determine if blacks had the mental capacity to fly and fight in combat. The Department's documented contention was that "these people" were not smart nor disciplined enough to pass the training; and should by some quirk of fate any survive training, they surely did not possess the courage or moral fortitude to face combat. Some believed the placement of the program in the deep south was only one of the many factors designed to contribute to its expected failure, although Tuskegee Institute had an established record of achievement in the Civilian Pilot Training Program.)

In addition to acclaimed Booker T. Washington, Dr. George Washington Carver, one of the world's foremost chemurgist and leader of Tuskegee's recognized research program in biological sciences, was a professor in residence. The presence of learned Negroes of noteworthy stature might have predisposed the white citizens of Tuskegee to greater tolerance of their colored population. In reality, the town was so harsh in its treatment of both permanent and transient Negroes, cadets longed to avoid it when making the nine miles trek from the air field to the Institute. The geography made that impractical, however, and on every commute they risked encountering die hard racists in the town of Tuskegee.

"Even though you were breaking no laws, you proceeded vigilantly. You never knew what to expect."

Whatever happened, the law was not going to be on Charles' side. He learned with the help of a classmate who happened to be from a well-to-do family in Montgomery to be extra careful and steered his way through the black community whenever possible.

With anticipation and trepidation, Charles and his new bride made their home in Tuskegee. Luckily they found a room on campus in Dorothy Hall for Frances. She got a job working as secretary to Dr. Kenny at the Institute's hospital. As she established her new routine, Charles entered the demanding world of the cadets. Housed in barracks on the Air Field, their regimen was long hard hours of instruction, grueling physical exercises and strict military discipline.

Contrary to the enthusiasm of the cadets, the Tuskegee program was considered a waste of money by many whites, including congressional and military leaders of the time. It was no secret these opponents echoed the War Department's sentiment that the Negro was not suited for combat assignments.

These nay-sayers were strikingly naïve in their shortsightedness. They failed to understand it took courage and fortitude for many Negroes to face and overcome imposing obstacles every day. The further irony is that patriotism and valor of the Negro soldier had been demonstrated on the battlefield in each of the country's past conflicts, but effectively purged from the pages of history. The feats of blacks who fought in the Revolutionary War, all black civil war regiments and the Buffalo soldiers were buried with these patriots. Now the Tuskegee Airmen had to rewrite the story.

Preflight training was the first phase all cadets entered. Military discipline was the order of the day. All gear had to be "shipshape" and the tuck for the bunk sheet exact, able to pass the bouncing quarter test, before morning calisthenics began at 6:00 am. After physical training cadets hit the books. Preflight training took place in the classroom. Topics included meteorology, Morse code signals for communication and E6B computer (circular slide-rule) computation necessary for flight planning. All of the theories and academic components needed for flying had to be mastered before climbing into the cockpit.

The early weeks proved to be a physical and mental endurance test. Physically, the most demanding challenge was the "cadet chair." If sitting straight backed at attention for long periods of time was hard, imagine doing it without a chair beneath for support. Charles felt his thighs and calves ache unmercifully when forced to "sit" in midair. The choice was clear; "short term discomfort for long term gain." It was reinforcement for the important lesson in keeping focused on the ultimate goal.

"Yes, sir; no, sir; no excuse, sir."

The cadet responses were similar to those from his fraternity pledging days, but now the stakes were higher.

Hours turned into days, days into weeks. It would take months to transform civilians from all walks of life into commissioned officers and combat pilots conditioned to face the harsh realities of war.

Five weeks of lower preflight training were followed by five weeks of upper preflight. The first phase was intended to screen out those not academically fit. Although other classes had as high as 50% wash out, in Charles' group all cadets passed. Whether due to college studies, performance, numbers needed to fulfill military requirements or a combination, Charles was moved up from class 43-G to 43-F, skipping upper preflight. In January of 1943, he was ready to move to the Primary Flight Training phase.

The long week of training was relieved by Sunday afternoon passes, granting cadets a few precious hours of free time. Most of the men were bachelors and free time to them meant the relentless but inspired search for available young ladies. Charles, having already claimed his bride, was spared the chase. He and Frances relished their time together; no moment was taken for granted. Whether sharing a box of cookies sent from home or a picnic under the elms, these afternoons and early evenings were savored, etched in memory to sustain them through the next separation.

Sundays with Frances made life in Tuskegee with all its rigors even more meaningful to Charles. He was preparing a future not only for himself, but for his family. He was a man with responsibilities he did not take lightly.

With Primary Flight Training came Charles' first airborne experience. The PT-17 was a bi-wing, open cockpit trainer.

Cadets used Moton Field, the grass airfield belonging to Tuskegee Institute, for this phase of training. With the help of Institute students, the airfield had been hurriedly completed for flight instruction in the summer of 1941. The instructors for primary training were black civilian pilots. These men were at the controls, demonstrating basic maneuvers including rolls, lazy 8's, stalls and the art of normal and emergency landings.

The world was a bit strange and disorienting viewed from above during Charles' first flight. After a few circles, his instructor pointed out significant landmarks.

"See the airstrip over there?" he asked over the sound of the engine and winds speaking into a Gosport Tube, the one way communication system which allowed instructors to talk to their students.

Charles glanced in the general direction indicated and nodded in reply, not at all sure of what was in the blurry panorama.

"Oh, yeah," he uttered.

I had to smile at this brief excerpt from my father's Tuskegee experience. Knowing him to be scrupulously honest and invariably proper in the use of English, if he muttered "yeah" even though he wasn't sure he saw the field, I can only conclude that he was indeed disoriented.

The PT-17, like most trainers, had dual controls and soon the cadets were performing the maneuvers. Instructors critiqued, advised and coached their protégés in the air and in debriefing back on terra firma. Though he mastered the mechanics of flying, Charles had not overcome a queasy stomach. It turned out the root of the problem was physical, not psychological. The flight surgeon recommended a simple solution: cut out fried foods for breakfast. After that, when he climbed and rolled, diving in and out of clouds, mind and body worked together and he began to enjoy himself.

The inevitable day, no matter how long awaited, seemed to arrive without warning. It was January 24, 1943. Just after landing, when it appeared the lesson was over, the order came.

"I want you to take it back up, make a pass around the field and come directly in for the landing," the instructor ordered.

Then the instructor stepped out and left Charles in the cockpit alone. A new energy pumped through his veins as he taxied back down the grass strip to take off position. The air about the plane seemed thinner. Charles took a deep breath summoning calm, applied power and raced forward.

When his aircraft reached flying speed, he gently eased back on the stick. The tail lifted and he was soloing!

As he climbed into the pattern around the field, a calm exterior belied the voice inside screaming.

"...I'm flying by myself." Banking into final approach, the voice offered a more subdued caution, "don't mess up now. I've got to land this baby," and finally, coaxing words of encouragement, "Come on. You can do this."

He maneuvered the plane to a gentle, almost perfect landing. Charles, fighting to suppress a Cheshire Cat grin, taxied back to the hanger where his instructor awaited the debriefing.

It was his first solo! The unforgettable milestone of all aspiring pilots had finally arrived and he passed!

From there, his education progressed more confidently. In each take off, Charles followed a specific plan. Aligning the aircraft into the wind, he advanced the throttle, used the rudder to keep the selected direction, and eased back on the stick when flying speed was reached, allowing the plane to soar into the sky.

In the propeller craft, the rudder provided control necessary to counter forces created by propeller rotation and engine controls were adjusted and set (throttle to give power, mixture controls for the fuel and air ratio, and pitch on the propeller). Checks assured everything was reading properly: engine temperature, fuel and pressure gauges for various systems. When ready, Charles released the brake, added throttle and started ground roll. There were things which determine the length of ground roll, but at the right speed, flight was inevitable.

The wing provided the lift surface. At takeoff, Charles applied the slight amount of back pressure to elevators to rotate his aircraft to a climbing attitude. At the right attitude and trim, he could take his hands off the controls and still climb. That was the science of flying.

Coming in for a landing was the reverse. Charles learned the correct balance between slowing the aircraft and adjusting the flaps to approach speed. Too much reduction meant a stall if he dropped below flying speed. He descended controlling the attitude to put the plane in landing condition. The wrong attitude could result in a hit and bounce. With too much speed he couldn't keep the plane on the ground. He learned the trick was to come down smoothly, kill speed until the wheels touched ground, and at that point diminish remaining power so the full weight of the aircraft settled down. As experience increased, Charles became more comfortable with the variables and began mastering the art of flying."

...Just to be able to go up at altitudes above all the noise and clutter of earth--it's something that's hard to put into words. It's a feeling of freedom, of not being bound.... It's what stuck with me and kept me at it."

While Charles was progressing with primary flight training, the first graduates of the Tuskegee program, the 99th Pursuit Squadron, were stuck at the TAAF enduring many months of delays by the still reluctant military leadership. They were generating enough red tape to keep these new black pilots out of the war they had so valiantly prepared to enter.

Among the white leaders at TAAF, Colonel Noel Parrish believed in the capabilities of the black pilots he trained and spoke earnestly for their activation. Parrish came to Tuskegee in May of 1941 to command the newly activated 66th Army Air Corps training detachment and followed the first graduates to Advanced Flying School, becoming Director of Training later that year and Base Commander early in 1943. Parrish replaced Colonel Frederick V. Kimble who showed greater concern for upholding the credo of segregation, civilian and military, than the progress of the Tuskegee program. Within War Department policies, Parrish's thoughtful nature and belief in fairness led him to implement practices to improve the quality of life for blacks at Tuskegee.

Charles' 43-F class, which would join the 332nd Fighter Group, had its first drop outs during primary flight training, but most moved on to Basic Flight Training. Basic was the first time the cadets would be assigned to white military instructors who were their trainers in the BT-13A at the Army airfield. Because they had been instructed to "train by the book," there was no concern that the black cadets were getting different or lesser preparation than their white counterparts.

Basic brought more complex assignments on the ground and in the air. For the weight and winds, Charles computed the speed at which the aircraft would lift. He tested his ability to maneuver the craft and its responsiveness. While he learned to master the challenges of the sky, Frances held her own on the ground, now living in a private residence. She worked by day and busied herself sewing and reading in the evenings. Charles' visits were not as frequent as desired.

Charles' father, sister and brother had each entered military service. Lewis Sr. was again serving as a chaplain, Ruth joined the Woman's Army Corps, and Lewis Jr., leaving college, signed up for the Signal Corp. Because of segregation, often blacks were assigned to Negro training locations regardless of whether or not their skills were needed. TAAF did not need additional Signal Corps officers, but Lewis Jr. was stationed there for a short time before reassignment to the Pacific Theater of operations where his skill was needed. This temporary assignment gave Frances an occasional opportunity to visit with him.

Advanced Flight Training in the North American AT-6 followed Basic, and while a few more fell by the wayside, most cadets persisted. Eglin Army Air Field in Florida was used for gunnery training.

"I reached 'expert' in aerial gunnery, but did not achieve that level of accomplishment with the 45 caliber handgun."

The lessons were direct omens of the missions which lay ahead and underscored the importance of mastering each skill needed for survival. Charles was doing well.

On April 15, 1943, the 99th finally shipped out to join the war in North Africa. It was a proud day for everyone at the Air Field. The cadets were filled with new confidence their hopes would become a reality.

Addressing the departing fliers, Base Commander Parrish observed, "You are fighting men now. Your future is now being handed into your own hands. Your future, good or bad, will depend largely on how determined you are not to give satisfaction to those who would like to see you fail."

On 30 June, 1943, Charles was a graduating member of Class 43-F, TAAF, SE (Southeastern) Flying Training Command. He received his silver wings as a single engine pilot and was commissioned 2nd Lieutenant in the Army Air Corp. Frances proudly pinned on his wings and Momma Nellie, who had come down for the special occasion, beamed through the ceremony. Eyes were moist. That day was unforgettable!

There was unmistakable satisfaction in Dad's voice as he recalled the event. Over fifty years later, I relived it with him and shared the feelings of accomplishment it represented.

Most families remained behind in the heart of Alabama, while newly commissioned officers left for the final phase of their preparation, Combat Training at Selfridge Army Air Field in Mt. Clemmons, Michigan. Now pilots, they had to go beyond to become fighter pilots. At Selfridge, three squadrons, the 100th, 301st, and 302nd, Charles' unit, were brought together to form the 332nd Fighter Group. They began training under

Col. Robert Selway, later relieved by Lt. Colonel B. O. Davis Jr., who had returned from battle in North Africa where he commanded the 99th Pursuit Squadron. Davis' presence evoked an allegiance not matched by any other commanding officer. All the pilots knew of his story. His father, B. O. Sr., was the first black general in military service in this country and B. O. Jr. was a graduate of West Point. They heard of the intense hazing he had endured at the hands of all-white counterparts at the Academy. He had been sentenced to exile in a world of silence during his four years there. Now, combat experienced, it was his job to mold the men of the 332nd into fighter pilots ready to go up against Germany's finest aerial combatants. Charles and the other men had great admiration for Davis.

The training in Michigan focused on combat readiness. The pilots learned about various weapons and combat strategies. The final challenges to surmount included gunnery, formation and night flying, and combat tactics.

By October the pilots were fully combat ready in the P-40L and the P-40N. That's when the decision was made for the group to fly the Bell P-39Q. It had the engine in the back and less horsepower than the P-40. In their enthusiasm, the pilots didn't complain. "If the crew chief can start it, then I can fly it," was their attitude.

As soon as circumstances permitted, Frances moved to Michigan. Once again they found a small room. Charles bought their first car, a Hudson Terraplane, and taught her to drive in Detroit.

Their time together ran out on December 22, 1943. Charles now faced the ultimate test. Three days before Christmas, his unit embarked by train to Fort Patrick Henry near Hampton Roads, Virginia. After several more days of waiting, he boarded the T. B. Robinson which joined the convoy of Liberty Ships departing the evening of January 2, 1944. For reasons of military secrecy, their destination was not divulged even to those being transported.

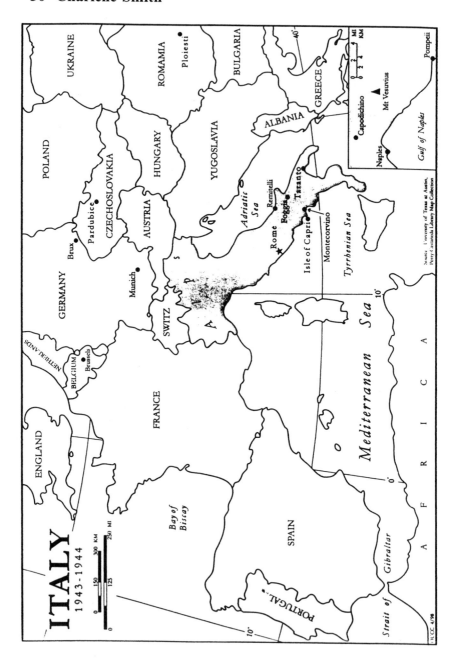

IV: World War II

1944

- The all-black 477th Bombardment Group was activated in January, 1944, and began training at Tuskegee Army Air Field.
- Almost 1,000,000 black men and women were serving in the U.S. armed services.
- Allied troops invaded the Normandy coast in northern France in June, 1944.
- In August, Paris was liberated after four years of occupation.

In December of 1965, the U. S. Army issued orders assigning a young soldier to Camp Casey near Souel, Korea. His wife of less than a year, a new mother barely out of her teens, was devastated by her husband's impending departure. Instinctively, she reached out for comfort and support. Across many miles, she phoned Frances.

"Mom I have terrible news."

Without pausing for a response, I lunged ahead.

"Bill has been assigned to Korea. He ships out in thirty days, right after Christmas. It's a hardship tour. The baby and I can't go."

The anguish in my voice underscored my firm conviction that something fundamentally unfair was happening. In a just world, separation would not be forced on a young couple just starting married life.

Of course, Frances knew better. Like many women, she had waited at home for someone she loved who went to serve the country in a foreign land. Frances, a veteran in her own right, accepted this assignment as a natural part of life for military husbands and wives. Nevertheless, her matter-of-fact reply shocked me.

"So, that's all you have to worry about."

I was dumbfounded; she hadn't understood. I tried to explain. Mom patiently informed me that far from terrible, this was to be expected. Rather than being upset, I should be grateful Bill wasn't going to Vietnam. She assured me the year would pass and Bill and I would most likely survive what in hindsight would be a relatively short separation.

I couldn't imagine how my own mother could be so callous. Of course, in hindsight she was perfectly right. Still, I can't help thinking she was not so calm and objective when she said good-by to Dad as he boarded the troop train leaving Michigan twenty-two years before. I suspect her heart ached as much as mine and innumerable others throughout time.

In late December, 1943, Frances left Detroit driving the Hudson back home to Champaign, Illinois, with the company of her half sister Sadie, as Charles began his journey to war. After shipping out from Virginia, he spent days at sea zigzagging across the Atlantic before the first sighting of the land when the convoy passed through the Straits of Gibraltar into the Mediterranean. From there, they journeyed along the northern coast of Africa, then turning north to dock in Taranto, Italy, on February 3rd. On land, the squadron boarded trucks for a road trip over the mountains.

It was slow going. The caravan had to negotiate narrow, winding roads which weaved up and down steep slopes across the arch of the boot in southern Italy. The cliffs were sheer with precipitous drops. Trucks, after climbing these hazardous roads, had to ease through cramped streets in small villages perched on the mountain tops. Images were a far cry from the U. S. countryside familiar to Charles and the sight of the lumbering motorcade must have been equally strange to the hilltop inhabitants.

Reaching their destination, the fliers made camp at Monte-corvino, south of Naples. The location was nothing more than an airstrip and adjacent row of tents serving as billets, mess and headquarters. After settling in, Charles and the others started the routine they would associate with life in the combat zone, patrolling Naples harbor to the Isle of Capri and along the coast. Ground time consisted of briefings, maintenance of equipment and aircraft, and waiting.

Not all flying assignments were associated with a combat mission. Airborne testing was required after maintenance to verify the plane's readiness. Charles was one of the pilots called on to do "test hops". Accompanying these activities and the eternal waiting was the ever present cup of GI coffee. Charles added liberal amounts of cream and sugar to make his more palatable.

The plane assigned was the P-39Q Airacobra, essentially a low altitude aircraft flown at 10,000 to 15,000 feet. Too slow for effective aerial interception, missions mainly involved harbor and coastal patrols to determine the movement of German and Italian forces.

"By the time we reached altitude to intercept intruders, they were usually back in Germany. It was frustrating."

Though airfields like Capodichino where the squadron relocated in early March were not a major objective for the enemy, they were not spared either. Nuisance raids were made by German aircraft aware of the American presence. Radar technology was relatively primitive and there was seldom advance warning. Night raids were the most common. Not long after Charles' arrival a raid succeeded in damaging twenty seven of his squadron's planes on the ground. In the aftermath of the attack, Charles recalled the rush to dig deeper foxholes. No one complained.

Night raids never became routine, but searchlights crisscross-ing the dark sky were part of life. So were British rations. Charles found powdered eggs to be the most objectionable item on the menu. "V-mail" from home was an eagerly awaited high point of each day. Letters from men in the field were censored to remove information that might disclose whereabouts and activities. Charles stuck to safe topics, conveying how much he missed everyone and looked forward to coming home.

After three months of patrol flights and enduring night raids, the 332nd heralded the arrival of the P-47D Thunderbolt at Capodichino. The replacement craft brought relief from the limitations of its under-powered predecessor and heightened expectation for greater involvement in the war. The unit was transferred from 12th Air Force tactical missions to the 15th Air Force for strategic tasks. In late May, the 332nd moved to Remitelli on the Adriatic side of the Italian peninsula, closer to enemy held territories. There a runway of pierced steel inter-locking planks was installed. Tents continued to provide all accommodations with the exception of an old farm house which served as briefing headquarters.

Following the move, Charles and his fellow pilots began bomber escort and fighter sweeps against German targets. As the Allies advanced north, bombers came up from Africa to bases in Italy, but they were getting their tails shot off over targets like Ploesti, so four single-engine fighter groups were picked for escort. The new assignment gave the 332nd the opportunity to apply their abilities against objectives on the ground and in air.

The P-47 was fine with B-24s, but not so good with the B-17s which could fly higher to avoid anti-aircraft fire. The fighters liked to be a couple thousand feet above the bomber stream to do their rolling S-turns, which allowed the greatest span of the horizon while matching the bombers' progress. Even when its supercharger cut in at 19,000 feet, the P-47 would become sluggish trying to get above the highest B-17s.

Facing combat regularly now, Charles did not allow doubt or fear to cloud his judgment. He and the other Tuskegee Airmen knew self doubt and hesitation posed a greater threat to well trained pilots than the enemy. They heard of pilots overly concerned about the performance of their engines who let apprehension get the upper hand, but these were exceptions. In the cockpit, Charles was guided by his training and untroubled by thoughts of his own mortality.

One Tuskegee Airman, who survived part of World War II in a German prison camp, expressed the same conviction fifty years later. At a college presentation at Ohio University, a young student in the audience asked if the pilot had ever been afraid during his assignments.

"If I ever felt fear, I would have climbed out of the cockpit without hesitation and returned to quarters," was the Airman's reply.

"Up there you're no good to yourself or anyone else if you have doubts and you had better understand that."

The other Airmen on the panel nodded their agreement. I looked at the student half expecting to see signs of disbelief on his face. Instead, there was revelation and perhaps a new source of strength to face his own battles.

The Airman provided another insight that day about his treatment as a prisoner of war.

"As hard as things were, there (in the camp) I was not black or white. Just another American pilot and officer afforded the same treatment as the others. That was better than I got when I was freed and returned to my own country after the war."

Like others in the audience, I was stilled by the significance of these words.

As much a threat as German aircraft were, engine trouble was often a more plaguing problem. Before computers, pilots relied on a finely tuned ear to distinguish normal engine sounds from those signaling danger. After days of persistent rain, keeping mechanical parts operational was a problem for the ground support crew who fought a continuous battle to maintain well-tuned engines. It was not uncommon to abort a mission due to engine problems, particularly after several days of rain.

On one occasion Charles was airborne and en route to his destination when he was forced to turn back because his engine wasn't running right.

The mechanics at the base were ace detectives when it came to discovering a problem, fixing it and returning the craft to the skies. The mechanics' ear was even more sensitive than the pilots' they kept aloft and they knew their craft so well, they could often diagnose a problem on approach before the plane even touched down. No sane pilot ever underestimated the value of his mechanic. On the contrary, ground support personnel were held in high esteem and rightfully credited with powers just short of the magic which kept the airmen flying. In the midst of aerial combat, Charles knew that in addition to his own skill, his fate was in the hands of God and his mechanic, to whom he entrusted his life.

The craft, pilot and mechanic were family. Just as any family member, planes were named, often after loved ones or significant interests, past or future. Some were decorated with provocative pictures or humorous slogans. Others reflected songs, dances or sayings popular in the black culture. Charles was assigned P-47D No. 280 and named his plane "Kitten." He chose the name for two reasons. First, it was his nickname for Frances and, second, it was also in honor of his mechanic, Nathaniel "Nate" Wilson, who kept her engine purring.

The days of the P-47 were short lived. As happy as everyone had been to see them come, they were even more delighted when they were replaced by the P-51C-10 Mustang fighters after six weeks. The newer aircraft had many advantages. One was operating at higher altitudes, easily climbing over 30,000 feet, which allowed the fighters to rise with the bombers above the range of most antiaircraft artillery. The P-51s were also much more maneuverable which had obvious benefits when engaging the enemy in dogfights.

"We would get into a scrap....zooming around up there in the air pretty close to each other at some pretty good speeds."

On July 4, Charles flew his first long-range mission in the Mustang (P-51C 42-103072, which also bore the name "Kitten"), escorting bombers to Romania. All the missions were long flights, usually five hours and more. On those flights, Charles found the cockpit small.

"You can sweat through a leather flight jacket sitting up there in the sun."

On long flights like that, he was glad to get off target and relax a bit in less rigid formation on the way back.

In September 1944, Charles was promoted to first lieutenant becoming a flight leader in the 302nd. Unpredictable by their very nature, the days of war nevertheless took on a rhythm and, strangely, a semblance of order. The day started before dawn. Plans were presented at 6:30 am briefings. Missions were posted and pilots received their assignments. Those on escort missions confirmed rendezvous time, location, altitude, course and fuel requirements. Backing off rendezvous time, pilots figured start engine, taxi and take off times and noted them in their flight log. When they got to the landing strip, the ground crew had the craft lined up and waiting. Starting at the nose of the plane, Charles and the others made the last minute walk around and checked the tires for leaks before getting strapped in with the aid of their crew chiefs.

After looking down the line and checking that everyone was ready, Charles as flight leader pulled out, followed by his wingman (the position he formerly held before moving up) and then the element leader and his wingman. They took off in pairs to expedite getting airborne. When both ends of the runway were used to get four squadrons airborne rapidly, it meant downwind takeoffs (something to be avoided with high winds) to get aircraft in place at the designated time.

Usually, each squadron would take off with 18 aircraft which included two spare planes. If everything went well as they climbed and formed up, the group leader would tell the spares to go back to base, but if anyone was having engine trouble, then they would go wherever needed. The commander of the 302nd was Captain Edward C. Gleed. After he became group operations officer, the squadron was led by 1st Lieutenant Melvin T. "Red" Jackson, then 1st Lieutenant Vernon Haywood.

P-51s had two drop tanks holding 65 gallons of fuel each, enough to support missions of four and a half to six and a half hours, depending on weather, altitude, targets and resistance encountered. Bombers were slower and their missions at times exceeded ten hours. In the first hour the big planes circled in low altitude staging areas until all were assembled. Often more than one fighter group was assigned to escort bombers to and from their targets deep in German territory. With a full fighter squadron deployed, there were four flights or sixteen planes in formation. When Charles flew escort, there were sometimes three or four squadrons protecting a bomber stream with as many as sixty bombers. The skies were darkened with aircraft.

Fighter pilots and bomber crews developed a special symbiotic relationship. After the arrival of P-51s with greater cruise efficiency, fighter escorts could stay with the bomber stream for longer periods at a time, but there were still "dead spots" where bombers were unescorted and more vulnerable to attack. The fighters knocked out antiaircraft guns and picked off Luftwaffe aces whose task it was to down the bombers before they could reach and eliminate their targets. Returning to base, the bombers were still at risk from German fighters who waited for escorts low on fuel to peal off before mounting their assault.

Successful bombing raids destroyed fuel, oil and chemical plants and supply lines which supported the German war machine. For quick aerial identification, many fighter groups painted the tail of their planes in bright distinctive colors and patterns. There were the candy-stripped 31st, the yellow-tailed 52nd, and the Checker-tail planes of the 325th. The gunners on the B-17s and B-24s loved it because they could easily tell who was friendly at high altitude over the target area. The 332nd came to be known as the "Red Tails" and made a name for themselves among the bombers, but the relationship did not get off on an easy footing.

The alliance between fighter and bomber pilots was based on shared objectives and sustained by mutual respect, two elements which in peace time had not existed between blacks and whites. Initially, bomber groups were not even aware there were black fighter pilots. With no frame of reference, they couldn't conceive of black men as pilots, let alone fighter pilots serving as their protectors. Skepticism about the ability of black men to perform this role not only existed in the field, but also was in the highest military and political offices.

As word of black escorts spread, disbelief turned to dismay and anger, early reactions by white bomber units to the presence of the Tuskegee Airmen. Fueled by bias from above, they expressed outrage that a few ignorant do-gooders would put the lives of white American soldiers in jeopardy by assigning the 332nd Fighter Group to escort them. Having come this far, the Tuskegee Airmen faced two enemies and one was American.

Another concern for pilots in WWII was the weather. Forecasting was a crude science. It was possible to take off in clear skies only to confront a number of weather obstacles. One was the dreaded jet stream which became very apparent when crossing the Alps while escorting bombers. Though not well charted at the time, the pilots learned that once caught in the stream, it was almost impossible to make forward progress and precious flying time was lost.

"Ten minutes would go by and you'd still be looking at the same mountain. You had no idea what in the world was going on."

When no headway could be made, the formations went to an alternate mission or turned back to base.

In the full squadron with four flights of four craft each, flying through clouds was tricky and there were a few occasions when the squadron was separated, but fortunately no midair collisions. Maneuvers in formation required close watch of the flight leader and most communication was in the form of signals from the leader. Kicking the rudder (fanning the tail) meant to spread out and wing up signaled to pull back together. Responding to maneuvers and signals, each pilot worked to hold his position in the element or flight.

Escorting fighters picked up the bombers inbound and for shorter missions stayed with them over target, climbing higher because of the flack (anti-aircraft fire). Coming back they stayed with the bombers until the "safe line" where chances of German planes pursuing were remote. On long missions one group flew penetration escort and another took target and egress support. When Charles flew his first mission escorting bombers to Munich, he felt like they were finally doing the job they had come to do.

The aircraft of WW II had limited navigational aids and while reference was made to instruments in flight (attitude indicators, directional gyros), they were unsophisticated and of minimal value in combat. With training, experience and intuition pilots had to determine whether or not to believe their gauges, or their instincts and senses in any given situation. The latter, referred to as "flying by the seat of your pants," was a carryover from earlier days of aviation when all pilots had was a magnetic compass and yaw string out on the wing.

The Army Air Corps provided a respite for air crewmen to get away from action at the front. After a defined number of missions, white pilots took leave at a rest camp on the Isle of Capri. The black pilots used a villa in Naples. During leave, Charles and several other Airmen opted for six days in Naples or three days in Rome. They took sightseeing excursions to Mount Vesuveus and Pompeii, but even among Italian civilians U.S. soldiers kept pretty much to themselves. In occupied territory, it was wise to maintain a vigilance. Along with entertainment, USO shows offered another temporary escape, the opportunity to relax, reminisce of home and enjoy an oasis of Americana in the distant land.

After a chance to recoup, Charles returned to action. Word of Tuskegee Airmen feats had spread and the bombers, so recently resistant to the idea of black pilots, changed their attitude. They now looked forward to seeing the Red Tails overhead.

"They knew when they had Red Tails flying with them, they had protection from the Germans they could count on."

Reputed to be a hard hitting group, the Tuskegee Airmen were known to hang in there and get the toughest job done. A disciplined group of fliers, they remained focused on their escort mission, even if it meant resisting the urge to chase enemy aircraft in search of aerial victories and personal glory.

"The leader of the 332nd Fighter Group (Col. Davis) instilled in us that our mission was to protect those bombers from enemy fighters....if we heard German aircraft in the air and they weren't attacking the bomb group, we didn't go off looking for them. We stayed with the bombers."

In time of war, enlightened self interest had spawned a new partnership.

Flying escort, it was everyone's job to watch for enemy fighters. Protecting planes flew out to the sides, at times crossing over the bomber stream, depending on where the threat might come from.

"Everyone was swivel neck...constantly looking."

On some missions enemy aircraft were never encountered and on others the Red Tails saw them, but only engaged them if they attacked the bombers. The first to spot the enemy called it.

"Bogie at 11 o'clock high."

The squadron leader designated which flight would respond and the flight leader took his four planes and turned into the attacker.

Charles recalled one August mission which began like many others. The assignment was to escort bombers of the 5th Bomb Wing to a Czechoslovakian oil refinery and Pardubice Airdrome, north of Vienna. As the bombers approached, several German aircraft managed to get off the ground and once airborne mounted an attack. They were over target when the advancing German fighters were spotted. Charles got the word to respond and turned his flight into the attack. One of the German planes, a Focke Wulf Fw-190, broke formation and he pursued. Before Charles knew it he was in the middle of a "dogfight." From training and instinct, Charles put his P-51 through dives, banks, and climbs taking evasive action while maneuvering for position. Combat ensued and skills and daring were tested as planes crisscrossed the skies fighting for advantage.

"We were over the local airfield. I remember seeing a hangar on fire out of the corner of my eye."

Executing a roll, Charles was able to get on his enemy's tail. With his wingman 2nd Lieutenant Roger Romine flying cover to protect his flank, Charles fired a burst which found its mark. The disabled plane lost control and began to drop from the sky. Following the plane's decent, Charles saw no parachute to indicate the pilot's attempt to escape. As he watched, the craft careened across the airfield and exploded in flames at its perimeter.

"Must have hit something in the controls. He took a couple hard evasive turns and went right into the ground."

After downing the Fw-190 Charles stayed low and out of the sights of enemy ground fire. Getting out, he saw a train pulling into a station and dropped his nose to make a firing pass at the engine, doing some damage to it. Romine lost Charles in the action and had gone up to rejoin the formation, but not before witnessing and confirming Charles' victory.

Charles rejoined the escort as the bombers cruising outbound from the target headed back to base. It all had happened so fast, maybe six to eight minutes of action. In the aftermath, Charles performed the textbook check of his aircraft to see if everything was okay. Those brief moments and his instinctive response were what all the training and preparation had been about. In the most challenging aerial combat, he had measured up. He was the one going home. The kill was Charles' first aerial victory. There had been hits and he was credited with disabling aircraft on the ground, but this achievement surpassed the others.

The 302nd's 1st Lieutenant William H. Thomas got another Fw-190 and 1st Lieutenant John F. Briggs of the 100th Squadron downed a Me-109 on that mission. Regrettably, Roger Romine was later killed in an on-the-ground plane collision following his 97th mission on November 16, 1944.

Days brought new missions. On September 8, in a fighter sweep over an enemy airfield at Ilandza, Yugoslavia, Charles damaged a number of enemy aircraft on the ground and was credited with destroying one.

Missions eventually brought a ticket home for Charles and others. For bombers the magic number at first was 25 and for fighters 50 missions. His assignment over Brux, Germany, on November 17, 1944 was just another long mission, five hours and 45 minutes, his 136th to be exact. This was higher than the norm due to the slow flow of black replacement pilots linked to strict enforcement of the policy of segregation. Over fifty of the missions had been long range escort. This one would be another, except when it was over, Charles' orders read ZI for Zone Interior which meant he would be heading home.

Before take off he posed for a picture next to "Kitten" with Nate Wilson, his crew chief, smiling by his side. The pilots and mechanics knew you could only fly one mission at a time.

After the snapshot, it was back to business and no time for distraction or thoughts about tomorrow and what it might bring.

The last mission brought a sense of relief and happiness, tempered by the specter of those who had not made it and those who still might not. Charles and others who fought with him were mindful of the high price of war, so there was no celebration in the field, only low key acknowledgment. The real homecoming parties took place stateside.

For all of its significance, that final mission on November 17, 1944 brought Charles a step closer to another fate. He survived the war and in less than a year would become a father. On November 13, 1945, I would make my way into this world and this remarkable man's life.

V: The Homecoming

1945-1948

- Following Roosevelt's death, Harry S. Truman became President on April 12, 1945.
- When Japan surrendered on September 2, 1945, Korea was divided at the 38th parallel with the Soviet Union supporting the northern sector and the U.S. occupying the south.
- The U.S. joined the United Nations.
- Freedom rides tested the 1946 Supreme Court ruling that segregated seating of interstate passengers was unconstitutional.
- The first swept-wing jet fighters, the Russian MIG-15 and American F-86, were introduced.
- Charles Yeager broke the sound barrier in October, 1947.
- In July of 1948, Truman signed Executive Order 9981 calling for the integration of the armed services.

In the victorious homecomings when WWII ended in 1945, ticker tape parades filled city streets and welcome home ceremonies took place in town squares all over the country. These were outpourings of love and gratitude the nation heaped upon its war heroes. And why not. The bravery and dedication of these soldiers had preserved freedom so fundamental and precious to democracy. Returning patriots were the object of admiration and respect.

Returning Tuskegee Airmen had a different story to tell. They had the record of achievement. To their credit were 150 air kills, including three of the first eight German jets (ME-262) over Berlin, hundreds of ground targets destroyed, over 1500 missions, 15,000 sorties, and the incredible sinking of a naval vessel by fighter gun attack. They owned the unequaled record of never losing a bomber under Red Tail escort to an enemy fighter. Sixty-six of their fellow pilots were killed in aerial combat, while another thirty-two were shot down and captured as prisoners of war. For his contributions to the war effort, Charles was promoted to Captain, credited with one FW-190 aerial victory and awarded 12 Air Medals.

"We shattered all the myths. Our record spoke for itself."

If the Tuskegee Airmen thought things would change when they came home, they were in for a rude awakening. Initially, there was room for hope. Shortly after processing through McGuire Army Airfield outside New York City, Charles was reunited with Frances in Illinois. The happy couple enjoyed a week's stay at a posh hotel on the Boardwalk in Atlantic City. Black and white soldiers shared this rest camp. Prior to these returning combat veterans, the only Negroes who frequented the hotel were maids, porters and waiters. Black and white eyebrows were raised at the sight of Charles and Frances enjoying the hotel's amenities. There was something to be said for a good bed and great food, gourmet dishes being a specialty of the resort. Real milk, eggs and especially ice cream were the favorites Charles enjoyed most.

These were short term perks and the Tuskegee Airmen deserved more. They were fully capable of flying the world's most technical aircraft. Their performance was up to any standards in the air.

"...a lot of what we fought for was an opportunity, to overcome having someone look at you and, because of your color, close a door on you."

They fought valiantly and victoriously, yet they received little acknowledgment and fewer awards and promotions than their white counterparts. Black pilots came home with 150 Distinguished Flying Crosses, eight Purple Hearts, Legions of Merit, and the Red Star of Yugoslavia, but a number of deserving Tuskegee Airmen did not receive the coveted

Distinguished Flying Cross in World War II. Citations leading to decorations were written based on mission records. Some records of the 332nd may have been passed over by an intelligence officer disgruntled over reassignment when the squadron was deactivated, but that was only speculation.

Back in the States black men who had trained hard and fought bravely for their country were expected to climb out of the cockpit and pick up mops and shovels, if they were lucky enough to find employment as janitors and ditch diggers. The burgeoning airlines industry welcomed white pilots but closed its doors to non-whites. Seemingly, the only ascent open to Tuskegee Airmen in civilian life was work as an elevator operator. Charles arrived home from defending his country in November 1944 to find America's attitude toward blacks unchanged. Passing notice may have been given to the uniform of black soldiers, particularly if the officer insignia was recognized, but the lasting impression was still based on skin color.

Lewis McGee and all three of his children had answered the call of duty, Lewis for the second time. They each lived through "the war to keep the world safe for democracy" to face the jarring reality of peace without justice. Charles was among the Airmen who wanted to continue flying. Their choices were few. He elected to stay in the service.

No more ready for integration than the commercial airlines, options within the Air Corps were few as well. Along with the other black pilots continuing in the service, Charles was assigned to replace white flight instructors at Tuskegee. Early in 1944, black cadets were being trained for the 477th Bombardment Group. The success of Tuskegee's fighter pilots heightened expectations of airmen in bomber training, who were still hoping to make their contribution to the war.

Assignment at Tuskegee would give Charles experience in the twin engine aircraft of the day: the AT-10, the TB 25J, a stripped-down B-25J which was a marvelous plane with big radial engines with a lot more power. The good news was he had a natural aptitude for instructing and was to spend the next year and a half in a job he thoroughly enjoyed.

He and Frances moved into a bungalow in the Carver Court addition, a two block area of small new single-family houses built to accomodate growth in the Tuskegee Institute community. They were anxious to furnish their new home, but Frances protested furnishings Charles preferred, thinking them too extravagant. Over her objections, they returned to Frank Tennile's Furniture Store in Montgomery and made the purchases. Afterward, she was very pleased. The furniture was not only beautiful, but durable enough to last a lifetime.

I should know, for many Saturday mornings it was my job to dust the intricately carved grapevines which adorned the dark rich wood.

Some people are blessed, or cursed, with the ability to find whatever good there is, even in fundamentally corrupt situations. Like McGees before him, Dad developed this knack and with it the ability to see in misfortune valuable experience preparing for what lies ahead. He and others with this inclination are not broken by adversity. Instead, they emerge with newfound strength and purpose.

No matter how debilitating the laws of segregation, some good came of them. For Charles and Frances it was lifelong friendships with the other black families which began during their time at Carver Court. As fliers, the airmen trained and fought together, and those who remained in the service were stationed together after the war. The families shared the waiting, happiness and tears of the war years. They became a major source of comfort and support for one another. Living, working and playing together at Tuskegee, close-knit bonds were formed. The airmen they didn't know personally were known by reputation. Names like George "Spanky" Roberts,

Daniel "Chappie" James, and Benjamin "B. O." Davis were well known and their achievements legendary within the Tuskegee families.

The town of Tuskegee was no more receptive to black airmen than before the war. Law enforcement officials made life difficult and even though Charles was cautious, it wasn't enough to prevent confrontation. He was accused of a traffic violation, arrested for speeding, and taken to jail. Making a statement in court, he told the judge he was in a line of five cars going the same speed and no one else had been accused of breaking the law. Charges were dropped.

Teaching at Tuskegee not only kept Charles flying, but also provided a channel to pursue his commitment to education and service to others. Albert Whiteside Jr. came to Tuskegee from Jones' Prairie, Texas. His life before he met Charles in December of 1944 had been farming under a strict regimen without much social life or time for reading and learning about the wider world. Not sure what course to follow, he knew he did not want to return to the farm. At the advice of another cadet, Whiteside sought Charles' help.

"Charles believed concern and compassion were important for any experiment to be successful. He welcomed me aboard and his friendship changed my life."

Whiteside successfully completed bomber training becoming an exceptionally capable instrument pilot.

Despite the overriding influence of segregationists in the military services, there were white leaders with foresight and commitment to fairness. Colonel Noel Parrish, still commander of Tuskegee in 1945, remained an outspoken champion of the move for equal treatment. Parrish formed his beliefs based on study and observation and challenged the status quo stating in a report submitted to the War Department: "Whether we dislike or like Negroes and whether they like or dislike us, under the Constitution of the United States, which we are all sworn to uphold, they are citizens of the United States, having the same rights and privileges of other citizens and entitled to the same applications and protection of the laws."

His experience and conviction not withstanding, preconceived notions of less open-minded leaders were deeply rooted and prevailed.

Military leaders were charged with the task of converting a victorious war machine to a scaled-down force, suitable for peace keeping. A victim of this transition, the 332nd was disbanded in 1945. Similar realignments were made leaving holes and gaps in groups in the "white Air Corps," but filling them with black servicemen was not thinkable since it would mean abandoning segregationist philosophy. Instead, the 99th and the 100th combined with two 477th medium bomb squadrons, units which had experienced numerous difficulties under bigoted leadership and never saw combat. Together they formed the 477th Composite Group under the leadership of Colonel B. O. Davis. The war in the Pacific ended before the newly formed group was deployed.

(The 477th Bombardment Group was activated early in 1944 when the accomplishments of 99th Fighter Squadron and 332nd Fighter Group could no longer be denied. Charles instructed pilots to fly the bombers as part of the 12-man crews including navigators, bombardiers and gunners who carried out bomber missions. Expectations for the 477th Bomb Group were high, both for contributions to the war effort and transition to civilian flying jobs afterward, but the war ended before the Group saw combat. Repeated problems stemmed from insufficient commitment to prepare and assemble the necessary elements. Under Colonel Robert Selway, Commander of the 477th Bomb Group, interest in sustaining segregation was the highest priority, leading to an odyssey of ill-conceived relocations from Selfridge to Godman Air Force Base, Freeman Field and back to Godman. Men of the 477th resisted efforts to deny their rights and in the " Freemen Field Incident" 101 were arrested and imprisoned in April of 1945 for refusing to sign an order restricting their use of the Officers' Club as stipulated in Army regulations.)

During their second stint in Tuskegee, Frances announced to Charles news of his impending fatherhood. She and Charles discussed the prospects of having their first child born in the deep south, and both felt the stigma of rigid segregation would forever be associated with an Alabama birthplace. Several months before my due date, Mom returned home to Champaign to await delivery and Dad stayed to continue twin engine instruction. They had been together less than a year and another separation wasn't easy, but Charles was flying and that part of the job he loved.

On November 13, 1945 word reached Charles of the birth of his daughter. He hadn't been on hand for the birth or twelve hours of labor preceding, which was as much the rule as an exception for military fathers. Frances' mother, Momma Nellie, was there to instruct the hospital staff and welcome her granddaughter. Three days passed before Charles could join them.

If events before had established his sense of purpose and duty, the sight of his tiny infant daughter, now a part of his life, served to further strengthen them. Responsibility to God, country and family took on new meaning when it included six pound, ten ounce Charlene Edwina McGee. Dad had chosen to make me his namesake. His large hands were more prepared to operate the controls of an airplane than to hold his daughter who seemed so small and fragile. Combat was perhaps less intimidating. Nevertheless, he doubled his commitment to make a good life for his family. Fortune smiled on me when I came into his safekeeping.

Soon after confinement, Frances was able to travel and we returned to Tuskegee. The family set up housekeeping there until Charles' reassignment in June of 1946. During this time, Lewis Sr. made a trip south to greet his new granddaughter.

After the war, he met Marcella Walker Harris during a visit to the Chicago public library. Among throngs of people, he spotted her behind the librarian's desk, which gave him the perfect excuse to approach her for assistance and introduce himself. As fate would have it, her offer of help lasted a lifetime. They had a lot in common; she too had been wed before and reared a daughter, Joan, alone when her marriage ended.

Charles had little contact with Lewis Jr. now and relations were strained. Charles couldn't put his finger on the consuming convictions his older brother developed, but he knew they were driving a wedge between them. The widening distance saddened Charles, but before it could be reversed, Lewis Jr. was sent to the Pacific theater.

Tuskegee Army Air Field was phased out, closing completely in 1946 due to force reduction and continuing dissatisfaction of black servicemen with treatment afforded them in the deep south. As a result of the segregated Army Air Force, few assignments were open to Charles at the end of the Tuskegee stint and it was inevitable he would be assigned to the reactivated 332nd Group. The 477th Composite Group had been deactivated. Now a full wing under the leadership of Colonel B. O. Davis Jr., the 332nd was based at Lockbourne Air Field, south of Columbus, Ohio.

At Lockbourne, the 332nd became known as the Black Air Corp. Most communities considered for locating the Group reacted by mounting protests and Columbus was no exception. But in this case the Corps prevailed. The performance of the 332nd may have planted the seeds for changing attitudes, but they had yet to germinate on a wide scale. Although a few temporary duty (TDY) assignments were made to white bases, most blacks in the Air Corps were assigned to Lockbourne.

At Lockbourne, life was much like in other bases. For every black pilot there were 10 other military or civilian black men or women on ground support duty who together were the backbone of the Black Air Force. The all-black force carried out its mission in isolation, away from the constant sting of prejudice. Housing on base was limited, however, forcing many families to deal with the bigoted community outside. Charles and Frances were finally able to rent a small house in a neighborhood on the far west side of Columbus. It was there I took my first steps and expanded my vocabulary beyond the first word, DaDa. Charles and Frances agreed to part with the family dog because the spaniel simply could not abide the intrusion of the newest member of the McGee family. To show her disapproval, she growled when she walked by my crib. It was most likely my first rejection, but Dad was there to teach me perseverance and Mom to steer me out of harms way.

Charles at twenty-seven was Base Operations and Training Officer at Lockbourne. A fighter squadron would have been his first choice, but Operations was management and considered a good assignment. One of Charles' responsibilities was check pilot for instrument flying. After pilots got their wings they had to be tested annually on their abilities to "fly blind," the term used when flying by instruments only. For this training, the cockpit was actually "hooded" so the view of the horizon was blocked. Check pilots would periodically review proficiency and sign off when standards were met.

To stay abreast of the changing technology, Charles and other check pilots required specialized training. In August of 1946 he and Chappie James reported TDY to Barksdale Air Base in Shreveport, Louisiana for a six week instrument instructor's course. Barksdale adhered to strict segregation of the races. Charles and Chappie did not readily accept the mold cast for Negroes, officer or not, at Barksdale. Between them they agreed to make a concerted effort to challenge the boundaries.

"We talked about it and decided while we're here, they would get integrated."

Charles and Chappie were among the thirty men from bases around the country who came for the concentrated program. Twenty-eight of them were white. The only other blacks at Barksdale were in a service squadron located on the far side of the field. People in this squadron were assigned to service work and were not allowed to use the BX (base exchange), the clubs or other recreational facilities.

"We decided in our free time we were going to do whatever was available."

They engaged in as many of the base's social and recreational programs as they could fit into their busy training schedule. When they showed up at the bowling alley, the clerk behind the counter attempted to deny them entry.

"You can't bowl here!"

"Where's the manager?" was their immediate response.

They bowled. In order to prevent a scene, the clerk acquiesced and the two become the first blacks to integrate the Barksdale bowling alley. To the chagrin of sponsors, Charles and Chappie entered a tennis tournament at the Barksdale officer club, winning the first round as much from determination as skill, before falling to more seasoned players.

Successfully breaching barriers erected by prejudice brought a sense of accomplishment and gratification. Sometimes it was even exhilarating. Once, entering the Officers' Club swimming pool, Charles had taken a lounge chair at pool side and Chappie was bouncing on the end of the diving board when the manager rushed in to stop them.

"You can't...."

The end of his sentence was drowned out by the splash Chappie made hitting the water.

"We did it. I don't know if they drained the pool later that day or what, " Charles reflected.

Similar incidents were repeated in many locales hundreds of times. Black servicemen continued to mount concerted efforts to force the hand of segregationists in military command.

Sometimes the objective was to purchase goods from the white BX, attend the movie theater, get a hair cut or enter the off-limits officers club. Always there was concern about what some senior ranking officer might do. These soldiers risked reprimands which could jeopardize career advancement, even arrest and court marshal for not obeying when ordered by whites to leave the premises, but they continued to a mount a campaign of resistance.

"We did those things to let folks know the time had come. You never knew when it might be to your detriment. We just did it."

Charles recalled other ways the establishment at Barksdale misused them. They had extra assignments not given to other officers in training. They were instructed to talk to black troops in the service squadron about VD (venereal disease). Although they should not have been asked to do it, they didn't refuse. It was an opportunity for the black enlisted men to see an officer who was one of their own. Charles understood their morale was low and, by his example, provided hope for a better future. White officers in command treated these troops badly, but Charles and Chappie did things to bring dignity and pride.

Negro media, like the Pittsburgh Courier and the Chicago Defender, played a prominent role in making the Tuskegee experience happen in the first place. The government's claim that the Negro was inept could no longer be supported after the war. The Tuskegee Airmen dispelled the stereotype. Monitoring the new struggle of their war heroes, the papers reported incidents of denied service and refusal to acquiesce to the rules of segregation with equal fervor. The strategies of challenging racial boundaries with peaceful but persistent confrontation took hold in the military and broadened the foundation for the civil rights movement.

When the US Army Air Force became the US Air Force in 1947, Charles went to Atlanta, Georgia, to take the examination to become a regular officer. His status at the time was still based on his initial entry into the reserves and call up to active duty in 1942. He never heard the results of the testing, but he was enjoying flying, so he stayed in the Air Force as a reserve officer on active duty.

With race the primary determining factor for military assignments, manpower imbalances were a persistent problem at Lockbourne and throughout the Corp. Charles understood the value of having a technical skill in addition to flying and, assessing his background and interests, decided to couple his pilot skills with maintenance expertise. In the summer of 1948, he applied for technical training as an Aircraft Maintenance Officer and completed the ten month course at Chanute Field in Rantoul, just north of Champaign, Illinois. As a nationwide training facility, Chanute was an exception to the rule, an integrated operation. There were a few restrictions even at Chanute, such as separate barber shops, but for the most part, the races worked and trained together. Charles was one of twelve officers in his class in the specialized program.

As anticipated, the aircraft maintenance and technical training gave Charles additional expertise the armed services needed. Timing too was right; things were beginning to change. When the Air Force, now a separate service from the Army since 1947, reactivated the 332nd Fighter Group and phased out the 477th composite group that had the B-25, there was no longer need for navigators at Lockbourne. However, the strict rule of segregation did not permit the reassignment of surplus black navigators to units where they were needed. To do so would have meant integrating the units against the Army's position. Air Force leadership, on the other hand, viewed the enforcement of segregation a poor use of manpower and too costly to maintain. A year in advance of Truman's executive order desegregating all branches of the military, Air Force officials led the way, selectively reassigning black servicemen from Lockbourne based on their qualifications.

In the final analysis, pressures brought to bear combined with enlightened self interest to bring an official end to segregation in the Air Force. The decision was an economic one. Despite differing opinions about its morality, segregation in the military was duplicative, inefficient and costly. Charles recognized that economic advantage was the impetus for change in the military. Just as in the private sector, the power of the "almighty greenback" was at work. Lacking a prevailing moral conviction, numerous obstacles were present to impede progress in desegregation. It was not all he hoped for, but it was a beginning.

The stage was set and in July of 1948, President Harry Truman signed Executive Order 9981 calling for the integration of the Armed Services.

WHEREAS it is essential that there be maintained in the armed services of the United States the highest standard of democracy, with equality of treatment and opportunity for all those who serve in our country's defense;

NOW, THEREFORE, by virtue of the authority vested in me as President of the United States, by the Constitution and the statutes of the United States, and as Commander in Chief of the armed services, it is hereby ordered as follows:

1. It is hereby declared to be the policy of the President that there shall be equality of treatment and opportunity for all persons in the armed services without regard to race, color, religion or national origin.

Truman's order gave the desired action the force of law. Henceforth, assignments would be solely based on qualifications. Under the new directive, deployment of the Air Force's most experienced Black officers and technicians, those of the 332nd, was accelerated.

Adding to momentous events, on September 6, 1948 Frances gave birth to Charles' son, Ronald Allen. As was the case with my birth, Dad was away on assignment, this time in school at Chanute. He had come home the weekend before, hoping to be on hand for the big event. Time ran out and Charles had to return. As soon as he got back to Chanute, a message was waiting for him. Frances was in the hospital. Before he could get permission and clearance to fly back to Columbus, he got another call telling him his son had been born. Now he had two children, a daughter and son, and even more reason to continue the struggle. No matter what its flaws, Charles believed in his country and the freedom he fought to achieve and preserve. He would teach his children to be strong and self disciplined and at the same time honest and respectful of others. He would make it a better place. One where Charlene and Ronald could grow up to inherit the promise of America.

VI: Desegregation

1949-1950

● The U.S. and western European countries formed the North Atlantic Treaty Organization (NATO) in March, 1949.
● The Soviet Union exploded its first atomic bomb in 1949.
● Members of the NAACP Legal Defense Fund challenged the constitutionality of school segregation.
● On June 25, 1950, the communist People's Republic of North Korea invaded the Republic of South Korea.

In 1949 when Captain Charles Mcgee finished maintenance training, he was assigned to an airfield in Salina, Kansas. As officer in charge of Base Shops for the Boeing B-29, Charles was stationed with the 301St Bomb Wing of the Strategic Air Command (SAC) located at Smoky Hill Air Base. It was his first integrated assignment.

Charles wasn't sure what he would encounter in Salina. The Air Force decreed the old ways over, but that didn't make it so. There were people who didn't want integration and their convictions were unchanged.

The job of Base Shops of the 301St Maintenance Squadron was to keep aircraft equipment operational. Minor work, such as fabricating or reworking parts, could be accomplished locally. When major repairs were needed, aircraft went to a depot. Charles commanded sixty or so technicians in various specialties. They ranged in rank from privates to master sergeants with two warrant officers and a lieutenant who assisted him. The work was technical and Charles had been trained for it. He knew the job and how to manage people.

Ribbons earned were worn on uniforms and the men knew Charles was a combat veteran, which may have helped. At work, things were on a good track.

Away from the job was a different story. There was no base housing. Servicemen with families had to find accommodations in Salina, but there was no place Charles could even rent, let alone buy. He was making progress in his career, but unable to have his family join him. Frances moved the children back to Champaign, Illinois, to wait while Charles lived in the bachelor officers' quarters (BOQ). Like it or not, this was the situation. He ate at the club, played bingo on Wednesday nights and did what he could to occupy time which otherwise would have been devoted to his family.

There were those on the job who didn't like taking orders from a black. Whether concerned about keeping their ratings up, getting promotions or for some other reason, they kept their feelings to themselves. Some may have been glad for change, but just as there was no open resistance, no overt show of support was offered either. No one rushed up with open arms.

Charles remembered one of the officers who made an overture. An operations officer like Charles at Lockbourne, he invited Charles to check out a plane with him.

"Hey, you're a pilot. Would you like to come over and fly this B-29?"

"Great!"

Charles was not passing up an opportunity to fly. The chance was a welcome change from the C-47Ds and B-25Js he flew to keep up his skills. The next time there was a craft to test, Charles went along as copilot. He was already qualified in a single and twin engine and was beginning to get a feel for flying the four engine B-29.

Flying at Salina gave him another opportunity for which he was grateful. Pilots needed proficiency flying and night flying. When a base aircraft was available and Charles was able to get the weekend off, after work on Friday he flew to Chanute. If the aircraft wasn't immediately needed, it could stay on RON (remain overnight) status, so Charles spent the night at home. It was one advantage of being a pilot, if the schedule allowed, but those times were too few and far between.

As a part of the ongoing readjustment of units after wartime, Air Force leaders decided they no longer needed Smoky Hill Air Base. The 301st Bomb Wing at Smoky Hill was assigned to Barksdale Field, Louisiana! In preparation for the move, Charles' task was to get all the machines unbolted from the floor, packed, crated and made ready for shipment. Knowing about family life for blacks in the south, he was not looking forward to joining the bomb wing there.

With preparing for shipment complete, Charles' orders arrived separating him from the Wing and sparing him the move south to Barksdale. Instead, he was to report to March Field near Riverside, California, as officer in charge of Inspection and Flight Test for the 22nd Bomb Wing and 1st Fighter Group. It is hard to imagine anyone happier to get a set of orders. Luck was on his side and Riverside it was!

Charles and Frances looked forward to being reunited and traveling west to California, the fabled land of golden beaches and movie stars. They had sidestepped the devil they knew in favor of one not yet introduced.

As the long journey to seek their new fortune began, Charles and Frances loaded their worldly possessions and two small kids in a 1949 Hudson for the cross country trek westward from America's heartland. Restaurants beckoned from billboards and motels displayed vacancy signs, but their messages were intended for white travelers. For non-whites, many stops were often made before finding food and lodging. In the meantime, hunger and exhaustion set in.

"It hurt to be denied a room at a motel when you could see the vacancy sign flashing in the window."

For Charles, the thought of sleeping along the roadside was more intimidating than the crudest rebuff, especially traveling with his family. En route they faced indifference and open hostility, and recognized them as a cost to bare for being black in America.

Years later, my husband and I drove from Champaign, Illinois, to his military assignment on the east coast. Although we stopped to eat wherever we chose and had no trouble finding a motel for the night, everything was new and strange. I had the eerie feeling I'd stepped off the edge of the known universe. Interstate highways turned to state routes, which gave way to country roads across uninhabited stretches of no man's land. The thought a dark-skinned stranger might not be welcome crossed my mind in 1965.

My parents' journey decades before was much more intimidating. In the best light, it should have been an adventure. Instead, it turned into an endurance test. The map showed the route, but did not warn it was a harder road for blacks to travel. Contemplating their journey, I felt connected to them and all our ancestors whose way was made similarly difficult.

I was too little to remember the trip to California, but as we grew, my brother and I learned the survival skills my parents had to acquire. I learned the process of finding lodging was a delicate and unpredictable one. I learned to read Dad's expression as he returned to the car and know whether or not we would be staying at that location for the night or pushing on to the next stop in the road. I learned that humiliating experiences could be borne with dignity and an unwavering sense of self worth, earning deepening love and respect. I learned the ultimate reward for patience and perseverance was sometimes a good night's sleep.

Whatever notions Charles and Frances had of California, when they arrived, tested and tired, the Riverside they found was as segregated as Salina, Kansas. There was no housing for Negroes anywhere near March Air Force Base. After repeated inquiries, a white fellow and his Indian wife offered them a nice place on the opposite side of town. It was on a hill with a steep, sandy approach. The man kept his chickens under the back porch. Sometimes the kids accompanied him when he stopped by to gather eggs.

It was a serene picture, this house on a hill with chickens scratching in the gravel yard. During the day, the children played in the sunshine and crisp white sheets waved on the clothes line. At night, Dad came home and we ate dinner and went for a drive or just did things together until it was time for me and Ron to go to bed. Afterward, Dad and Mom would sit at the kitchen table or outside under the stars and talk. It was a "normal" family life, not to be taken for granted.

At work things were "normal" too. The Air Force was moving to consolidated maintenance control. Rather than each squadron having its own inspection and flight testing, management was being centralized. March Field had a bomb wing and a fighter group. Reporting to Charles were flight test officers from these units. He was still doing proficiency flying in C-47s or whatever they had available at the base. March Field had C-47s for depot runs to pick up supplies or transport personnel. There were also aircraft to move the commander around and take care of other official travel.

At headquarters, Air Force initiatives were being drafted. Personnel were being selected for overseas replacements based on the number of months back in the States from combat assignment. There was a need for maintenance officers in the Philippine Islands. Charles, having returned from Europe in November of 1944, was high on the list to be rotated, even though he had been at March Field less than a year.

The decision was made to move the fighter elements at March Field to George Air Force Base on the high desert of California. With his fighter background, Charles was initially slated to go. Because of the overseas staffing initiative and his senior position as a maintenance officer, his orders were changed to the Philippines. The Philippines was not considered a hardship tour and families were allowed to accompany assigned servicemen. Once "in theater" (the term for arrival at an overseas assignment) application was made for family travel and he quickly completed the necessary paperwork.

Two developments affected Charles shortly after his arrival in May, 1950. The first had to do with an action known as the Johnson Purge. Johnson was the Secretary of Defense charged with force reduction to reverse the build up which had supported the war. Pilots were among those affected by the draw down. After Charles reached Clark Field, he received orders taking him off flying status. This was a stunning development, however he opted to remain in the service accepting a non-flying position for which he was qualified. Since the maintenance officer slots had already been filled, command personnel took a look at his record, saw he had been an operations training officer and the next thing he knew, Charles was in the base operations and training section again, this time as assistant base operations officer.

The second development occurred while Charles was adjusting and waiting for Frances to join him. The North Koreans crossed the 38th parallel, becoming the aggressors in a conflict with South Korea. The U.S. backed the United Nations resolution in support of South Korea, responding with an immediate build up. P-51 fighters were at once put back in service and assigned to a fighter group.

"I went over to the Philippines in May and it was in June the Korean War broke out."

He recalled the rapid succession of events.

"By the end of July, the 31st to be exact, I'm in Japan at Johnson AFB picking up a P-51D and flying into combat."

Just that fast, family travel was canceled and Charles was moved from his operations assignment to the 67th Fighter Bomber Squadron where he would fly interdiction in Korea, first from Ashiya, Japan, across Tsushima Strait from Korea, and then from bases located on the Korean peninsula.

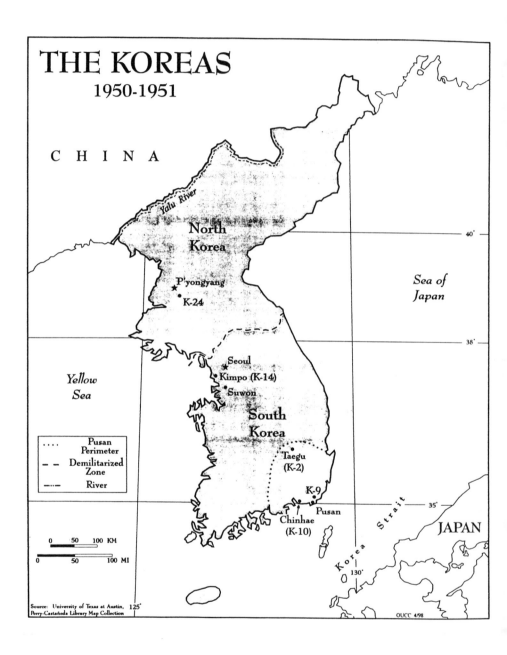

THE KOREAS
1950-1951

VII: The Korean War

1950-1951

- Both East and West possessed nuclear weapons vastly improved over the first atomic bombs and long-range bombers with increased capability to deliver them, creating an effective nuclear deterrent.
- In 1950, Senator Joseph McCarthy launched his crusade against internal subversion, a platform adopted by segregationists opposing the developing civil rights movement.
- General Douglas MacArthur led United Nations forces in a campaign to recapture Seoul, Korea.

For most of history, man's thought of flying was mythological musings. For many, it became something to avoid and for a few, a way of life. Even for the veteran flier, no two flights are alike. Wind, weather and weight combine with many other variables to make each a singular experience. In the early years, much of flying was experimental. With experimentation came greater understanding and technological advances, but technology did not change key determinants in overcoming the earth's pull. The basics were still the things Charles learned in pilot training.

From November, 1944, to July of 1950, Charles had not set foot in a P-51. Since jet planes were not in position to support the Korean offensive, P-51s were quickly pressed into service. Pilots now accustomed to the F-80s had to recall techniques in maneuvering the prop driven power plant.

The P-51s had main gear and a small tail wheel. At take off speed, there was risk raising the tail too high could nose the plane into the ground, but this wasn't new; the aerodynamics of flying the P-51 were fundamentally unchanged. Though increased power gave later aircraft impressive capabilities, the principles were the same. Charles mastered the technique and progressed in experience, skill and rating in a variety of aircraft becoming a senior pilot with the prerequisite seven years in grade and 1,500 hours of flying.

Between take off and landing, Charles enjoyed tranquil, almost serene, moments during flight. The clear vista of open skies and the curve of the earth's surface at the distant horizon were marvels to behold. On evenings with good visibility, the setting sun painted a breath-taking panorama. A new perspective on the world was introduced.

Charles on occasion took a camera on board in an attempt to capture these scenes. Pictures were a distant second to actually being there. For him flying was a natural high and once hooked, it was not something he could walk away from.

"Up there above 30,000 feet with the earth below and the canopy of the heavens above, you realize you are a speck, a grain of sand in the grandeur of the universe."

In 1950, the career that kept him flying conveyed Captain Charles McGee into the Korean conflict. Once again his training and skills as a combat pilot were called upon to defend against those who threatened the peace and security of U.S. Allies.

In the Cairo Declaration of 1943, WW II Allies pledged that Korea, a Japanese colony since 1910, would become a free and independent state. When Japan surrendered in 1945, Korea was divided at the 38th parallel with the Soviet Union allied with the northern sector and the U.S. in the southern sector.

In 1946, the Soviet Union opposed a United Nation's (UN) decision to hold free elections throughout Korea. Elections held in the south created the Republic of Korea (ROK) on May 10, 1948 and the U.S. withdrew its occupying forces. At the same time the Democratic People's Republic of Korea was established under a Communist regime in the north. Both the North and South Korean governments claimed rule over all Korea and the scene for conflict was set.

According to U.N. and U.S. observers, North Korean infantry and tanks crossed the 38th parallel on June 25, 1950. The U.N. Security Council adopted that same day a resolution calling for the immediate cessation of hostility and the withdrawal of North Korean troops. The Soviet Union was absent from the Council and Yugoslavia abstained from the vote. In response the Soviet Union declared the resolution illegal and asserted that the North Korean offensive had been provoked. A second Security Council resolution, two days later, asked for member assistance in repelling the armed attack on the R.O.K. President Harry S. Truman ordered U.S. air and naval forces to give cover and support to South Korean troops. Orders for Charles' unit were among those issued.

Different from the escort missions of WW II, the main thrust of air support early in the Korean War was interdiction. U. S. air power was aimed at supporting ground troops and stopping the North Korean advance. Interdiction involved taking out ground targets or stopping troop movement. In Europe, Charles usually flew one escort mission a day. He flew more frequently in Korea.

"With interdiction, as long as there were bombs and fuel, weather permitting, we were flying constantly--often two and on occasion three missions a day."

Charles' units' P-51s, now designated the F-51, carried bombs, rockets and napalm. When ground troops were in trouble, it was the job of the fighters to strafe enemy positions on the ridges and in bunkers. True interdiction took place behind enemy lines. Targets were bridges, truck traffic, supply trains and anything else that would halt transportation or slow the progress or re-supply of hostile troops.

Early in the conflict, jets desired for air superiority were not readily available. The F-80 and the first new swept wing jet, the F-86, designed for this type of role, weren't in position overseas, so the F-51 carried the early effort.

"We were all over the place, flying interdiction missions against bridges, trains and trucks. I expended lots of bullets, napalm and rockets to stop supply and troop movements. The North Koreans were firing as much at us as we fired at them."

After crossing the 38th parallel, the North Koreans moved south quickly toward Pusan almost pushing defending troops into the sea. For the first few days, the 18th Fighter Group squadrons flew aerial attacks from Ashiya, Japan until the Corps of Engineers could build an airstrip within the Pusan Perimeter. There ground was leveled and rice paddies filled to allow a pierced steel planking landing strip to be constructed. Each strip was given a number preceded by K for Korea. K-9 was the Pusan base. Pilots were selected for two squadrons of the 18th Fighter Group, the 12th and the 67th, Charles' squadron. Charles was in the first unit flying support from K-9.

"I flew to the K-9 strip to check on construction progress and spent the night under the wing of my plane."

While the F-51 was essentially the same as it was in the second world war, in place of wing fuel tanks it now carried napalm. With internal fuel, including a small fuselage tank behind the pilot, flying time was about two and a half hours at low altitude.

The North Koreans did not have a substantial Air Force. There was little aerial resistance to early interdiction over the southern region. To counter the allied air initiatives, the North Koreans were throwing heaviest fire from emplacements overlooking valleys.

In the fall, when China entered the war, U.S. pilots began to have air opposition and F-86s were needed. American jets established air superiority along the Yalu River south to Pyongyang. Several U.S. pilots became Aces shooting down Chinese MiGs when they intruded into South Korean air space. Charles didn't run into air opposition, the biggest hazard was a lot of antiaircraft artillery, firing back at him from the ground.

During a mission against Kigye hillside gun emplacements on September 16, four fighters were attacking targets. Near the end of the run, Charles was firing at the guns overlooking a valley on the north side and tracers were coming back at him. He was hit in the wing by incoming artillery, out away from the cockpit. Charles knew right away it was probably a 20 millimeter shell. He felt a thump and looked over to see fuel streaming from the plane.

"I didn't know exactly what it was. I felt something. How much, how bad I couldn't see."

Charles maneuvered out of the range of fire to get to a safe area, then climbed to clear the ridges. One of the wing men followed him.

"It wasn't really an escort, but he stayed with me in case."

If Charles had to bail out or crash land, the other pilot would be able to pinpoint the place. The engine hadn't quit. The wing and the tail hadn't been shot off. Control surfaces were operating normally enough to get back to base.

"Fortunately I made it, but the aircraft required major repair. It had to go to the depot for a wing spar change."

After the United Nations counteroffensive in September, the group flew out of a forward strip in Pyongyang as the Allied Army pushed toward the Yalu River. When the Chinese intervened in November, they then operated out of the main strip in Suwon. MIG-15s entered the war, but Charles and his unit didn't see many of them because most jets were flying at high altitudes.

At Suwon, as UN forces increased, pilots from Australia joined the effort and the South African 2nd Squadron was attached to Charles' Group. He and other men in his unit gave the South African flight leaders theater indoctrination before they assumed missions. Attitudes of apartheid in their homeland were not manifest in Korea and the two units worked well together.

"I actually made friendship among them from the commonality of flying and fighting side by side."

There wasn't a lot of chatter between men during a mission. Other than dealing with the controller, or occasionally the front line forward controller when Army units were involved, they observed radio silence. Artillery markers were used to identify target areas; that is how information was passed once airborne.

"When you see guys talking with their oxygen mask off in the movies, that's all movie stuff. We didn't operate that way in combat."

Before the missions, the intelligence officer briefed the fliers on where there was enemy fire and what they might expect. When the pilots returned from the mission, they recorded what was accomplished. Sitting with the squadron intelligence officer and reviewing the mission, they discussed what was observed and accomplished, and how much ordinance had been expended. Debriefing had two objectives: documenting what happened and gathering more intelligence. Information about truck traffic, rail traffic or troops observed was reported up the chain of command after debriefings. Hot news, such as a truck convoy, called for a turnaround mission heading right back out. As pilots passed certain milestones or did something noteworthy, the intelligence people recorded the event and passed it through channels to headquarters. From these reports, recommendations for commendation were issued.

When not flying combat missions, Charles attended to his responsibilities as squadron maintenance officer. His squadron commander, Major Louis Sebille, who gave his life destroying a target, was the first Medal of Honor winner in Korea.

"Our CO, Major Sebille, was fatally hit by anti-aircraft fire near Hamchang and crashed his Mustang into a concentration of enemy ground troops, for which he was posthumously awarded the Medal of Honor."

The war effort had to go on and, with his loss, seniority of officers determined reassignments. Each officer in the leadership hierarchy moved up. The operations officer, Major Arnold "Moon" Mullins, became commander. As maintenance officer, Charles became operations officer and another took his place, 1st Lieutenant Daniel Leake Jr.

In November of 1950, Charles was given a spot promotion to major. It would be officially confirmed early in 1951. In January, he completed the 7000th mission flown by pilots of the 18th Fighter Group since deploying from the Philippine Islands, a milestone reported in military news. Major McGee went on to complete 100 combat missions, flying his final mission on February 20, 1951, and earning several Air Medals and a Distinguished Flying Cross (DFC) for his contributions in the conflict. General Partridge, Commander of the 5th Air Force, came to the base at Chinhae to pin on the DFC.

His tour of duty in the Korean War completed, Charles headed away from his second fighter combat experience.

VIII: The Boys of the 44th

1951-1953
- In November 1952, Dwight D. Eisenhower was elected President of the United States.
- In 1953, Chief Justice Earl Warren was appointed to the Supreme Court.
- On July 27, 1953, Korea signed the truce agreement setting the stage for a negotiated peace settlement.
- Britain introduced turbo-prop powered air transports and pioneered jet airline service.

After Korea Charles returned to Clark Field in March and was assigned to the 44th Fighter-Bomber Squadron. It was the squadron of the 18th Wing that remained in the Philippines and he was glad for the assignment. The 44th had two jobs, air defense and refresher training for pilots called to serve in Korea. Charles was first assigned as operations officer, but a month later became squadron commander. The Clark Field years in Angeles, Pampanga, PI, proved to be exciting for a number of reasons, high among them was transitioning into jets.

Charles' love of flying was elevated to new heights with his introduction to jets. First time in the T-33 jet trainer, the pilot in charge of the flight had Charles read the tech order, fill out paperwork and shoot a few landings. Afterwards, the instructor discovered Charles had never before been checked out in a jet. He was amazed. Charles was so at ease in the new craft he had assumed the flight was a standard recheck. More than a great experience, to Charles jets were great fun. He piloted the Lockheed F-80.

"I loved jets from the first roll."

The best one word descriptor for jet propulsion is power; in two words, tremendous power.

"To think of jet flying, you've got to think of blowing up a balloon. You let it go and it shoots around the room. That's the concept exactly."

Except it's millions of balloons which have to be controlled. There is no torque (pull to one side due to propeller rotation); for the first time he could go to full power and, if all signs were go, release the brakes for flight.

"When you have more thrust, you can do things you couldn't even begin to assume.... You're dealing with power and a system that gives you even more power when you add 'afterburner' capability."

There was a thrust to weight ratio to be concerned about. There were adjustments to make. Charles learned the speed and characteristics of the new craft. Their potential was awesome, and now with ample power to rotate to an almost vertical climb.

"It was a mighty fine time," Charles reflected.

Frances and the family joined him at Clark Field. Base housing was available and Charles' rank and duties qualified them for a modern spacious home. In the Philippine economy, the American dollar went a long way. With pilot's pay on top of base pay, the McGee's were well off. They had a maid, Deloris, and a yard boy. Deloris also helped look after the kids. They probably would have had a cook too, except Frances insisted on keeping that task. She drew the line when it came to somebody else taking over her kitchen.

In the Philippines, Charles' leadership abilities had a chance to thrive. He was focused, disciplined, hard working and willing to make the tough decisions and be held accountable. Even though Charles was their leader, the men knew he was not asking them to do anything he wouldn't do. When needed, he rolled up his sleeves and worked along side them. The pilots under him admired and respected him.

To gain acceptance, it wasn't enough for blacks to simply meet expectations. It took exceptional contributions to break down racial barriers. Even then, the door only opened for one person at a time. Charles could have been resentful for having to prove himself above and beyond the norm, but he chose instead to have a degree of optimism. He dealt fairly with the men under him, most of whom were white. He sought their suggestions, allowed leeway for independent action, congratulated improvement and rewarded success. Charles knew their eyes were on him. If the call to battle came, they had no doubt he would lead.

Most of the flying between 1951 and 1952 was air defense missions for Formosa in the F-80s. Pilots of the 44th flew up and down above the rooftops of the capital city of Taipei showing a strong presence and the people there loved it.

Fighter pilots were a close-knit group. They worked hard and played hard, and often partied together. Their gregarious nature had been evident right from the start. Charles recalled stocking the refrigerator with staples in anticipation of his family's arrival and returning home to find meat and eggs sitting on the kitchen counter. His squadron members rearranged the refrigerator to make room for the beer and these low priority items no longer fit.

True to reputation, the fliers lived to party. Every Saturday night they took turns hosting. There was Bill and Polly Pollock, Ann and Jim Garrott, Jack and Amy Stykes, and the Brooks (Marina and Nelson) among others. Their raucous marathons started after dinner and lasted until those who couldn't make it home "crashed" where they fell and die-hards, still swinging when the sun came up, had breakfast before heading out. One unforgettable hangover let Frances know early in the game she could not "hang" with the serious drinkers. From then on, she nursed a drink for hours and was one of the sober ones in the bunch when the party broke up.

Charles enjoyed the close ties between the men and their families. Whether house parties, at the officers club, on the baseball field or side trips to Hong Kong, they had a good time together. They shared a special bond.

"We're the boys of the 44th. Who the hell are you?"

That was the greeting they had for anyone bold enough to approach the high spirited group. They had been known to "turn the club out" a time or two. As in work, Charles rolled up his sleeves and joined in, at the same time keeping the lid on. He knew these times played an important role in melding the unit, but if things got out of hand, it could undermine rather than strengthen the bonds they needed to work as an effective fighting force.

Though Deloris kept Ron and me out of the way when the party was at our house, I had brief glimpses of pretty women with red lips, bare shoulders and tropical flowers in their hair. The men were strong and boisterous and everywhere people circulated talking, telling jokes and tall tales, the sound of their laughter rising over the music.

They shut out worries, at least for the moment, and enjoyed themselves. Tomorrow the men might be called to the battlefront, but tonight they were young, alive, invincible and making the most of it.

The years in the Philippines were carefree times for all of us. I loved to climb the clothes pole and perch on the top. Mom tried to keep me down for fear I would break a leg. Dad assured her it wasn't a problem. I was just being a kid and kids grow up, even after a broken leg.

When it was time to learn to swim, Dad offered a few pointers then threw me in the deep end of the pool at the officers club one sunny afternoon. Fighting to get back to the surface, I thought I was going to die. I remember gulping for air, thrashing for dear life and Dad calmly instructing from pool side.

I learned to love to swim and Ron, who must have observed the whole thing, learned to stay away from Dad when we were near the water.

To escape the heat of Angeles and Clark Field, the family (which included Deloris) would vacation at Camp John Hay in Baggio high in the mountains. The road to Baggio was a long, winding climb with steep cliffs on the side. From the window of the car only inches from the edge of the road, it was frightening to look into the plunging view below and a relief to emerge at the bungalow in the clouds, where we would relax and enjoy the cool mountain air for a few days before making the hair-raising journey home.

On January 14, 1953, one month after Dad's thirty-second birthday, a baby sister, Yvonne Gay McGee entered the scene. Given the date of her birth she was conceived not long after Frances and Charles were reunited after Korea.

I can't help thinking the blessed event was related to the aftermath of one of those infamous parties the fighter pilots were so well known for. Speculation aside, I carry the scar to show for another memorable event in the Philippines.

Teaching me to ride a bike, after a few trial runs on flat ground, Dad took me to the top of a drive, pointed my bike down the long paved street and let go. Part way down I was enjoying the rush of the wind in my face, when I realized I didn't remember the first thing about stopping. At the bottom of the hill, my best option was to bail out. I blew the landing, however, and split my knee on the curb in the fall. I can still see the pink flesh laid open and the white center which I assumed was my knee bone. The next thing I saw was Dad coming down the hill. Somehow he managed to carry me and my twisted bike home and reassure Mom it was nothing a few stitches wouldn't take care of. Among other things, I learned to be daring from this man.

While families were going about the business of everyday living, there was also the serious business of air defense conducted by the servicemen stationed in the Philippines. Radar kept track of air traffic and all planes had to be identified and cleared. Pilots were always on alert and would "scramble" at a moments notice to investigate suspicious aircraft movement. Pearl Harbor was not forgotten and never to be repeated! Announced and unannounced exercises, conducted day and night, tested readiness and keep response time at minimum required levels. The shriek of sirens and spectacle of men running to their aircraft was a common sight.

Ground threat was less a concern, but a dissident group known as the Hucks populated the hills and would descend to harass villagers from time to time. Youngsters were warned to stay within the fenced base perimeter unless accompanied by their parents or other adults. Despite the presence of the Hucks, Charles did not isolate his family from the Philippine people or their culture. He saw the overseas tour as a good learning opportunity and we left the base to shop in Angeles and attend public events.

I kept my eyes open for Hucks, concerned I might be kidnapped, carried away and forced to work as slave labor in the hills, never to see my family again! Like most kids, my rather dramatic imagination was working overtime. At an early age, I had learned the value of preparedness from Dad and conjured up numerous escape strategies just in case.

More frightening to me than the Hucks (probably because I never actually saw one of them) were the Flaggalanties who prostrated themselves on Easter holidays to make atonement for the sins of their families. These men covered their faces in shrouds, placed wreaths of thorns on the heads and, baring their backs, paraded through city streets. Some dragged heavy crosses made of mammoth timbers and others whipped their own flesh with glass studded leather straps. Young children struck them about the legs and ankles with switches, adding insult to their self inflicted injuries. The sun beat down on this painful drama and sweat and blood mingled on their bodies. I

*was sad for these men and frightened by them at the same time.
I also hoped their families would try harder to behave in the
future.*

*Throughout our stay in the Philippines, Dad demonstrated a
healthy interest in the political and cultural events surrounding
us. Whether servants or leaders, he treated Filipino natives with
respect, by example modeling good global citizenship. Curiosity
and tolerance were part of the legacy from formative years
lived in another country.*

Reptiles and insects were fearsome in the tropical climate.
Snakes were formidable, but even the twelve foot king snake
which took up residence under our porch didn't hold a candle
to pie-sized spiders that hung on screens and climbed the walls
of the car port. Charles tried to dispatch a particularly gruesome
one with his sandal. The spider simply lifted two legs, repelled
the sandal as a mere annoyance and continued on without
missing a step.

*A serious case of arachniphobia was another part of the
legacy from those years in the Philippines.*

At Clark Field, Frank Borman, a West Pointer and 2nd
Lieutenant in the 13th Air Force, was assigned to Charles'
fighter squadron. Borman had been taken off flight status due
to a broken eardrum suffered at Nellis Air Force Base and the
flight surgeon was hesitant about the possibility of reinstate-
ment. Grounded, but determined to fly again, Borman sought
assistance. Charles, judging him to be a good officer, agreed to
help and arranged to take Frank up. The flight surgeon carefully checked and documented his medical status before and after
the flight and the successful experiment proved Borman could
be returned to flight status. The suspension was released.

Later, convinced of his sound performance and exceptional
abilities, Charles gave Frank Borman an outstanding rating
which was challenged by his superior reviewer on the grounds
such ratings were reserved for higher ranking officers who
showed potential to be wing commanders. Charles stood by his

convictions that officers should be rated among their peers and did not change the rating. History proved him right and Borman went on not only to fly, but ultimately to join the elite realm of astronauts.

Of Charles, Borman observed.

"He was a wonderful leader, a great pilot and a dedicated patriot. I have considered it as a blessing that I was able to serve under him and observe his leadership in the formative years of my career."

Formation flying wasn't invented with jet airplanes, but the leap in power and speed took it to a whole new dimension. It is one thing to control a complex, costly machine traveling at explosive velocity and still another to do it within a few feet of other aircraft speeding along beside.

"The easiest (position) is to lead, because the leader just flies."

Formation flying combines knowledge of aircraft and aircraft maneuvering with constant vigilance and judgment. It's the wing man, left or right, who must work to stay in position. If the leader turns right, the wing man on the left goes up on the high side. If the leader turns left, he's on the low side. There are options; in a right turn, the left wing man may opt to stay level (echelon) accelerating to hold his place relative to the leader. The process is reversed in the roll out.

The "four finger" used in World War II was the standard fighter formation. In the four finger, the array of aircraft resembles the way extended fingers of a hand line up. The lead aircraft is out front and on his sides are his wing men. Whatever the leader does, the wing men adjust to stay in position. To maintain position means pilots have to continuously alter power. The outside man has the farthest to go and a mistake in judgment will pull him out of line.

From certain vantage points, aircraft in formation appear to be wing tip to wing tip and in a tight formation wings are actually overlapping on a different horizontal plane. There is also the "diamond" formation with one man flying the "slot" location, a bit under and behind the leader. The pressure is on all pilots in formation flying and the experience is exhilarating.

"There is nothing quite like the thrill of low-level formation aerobatics. Adrenaline and sweat flow freely as pilots flash through team maneuvers. Many dream about it, but very few have the right stuff to live it."

The diamond formation, not used in combat, was popular in air shows. At shows in the Philippines, spectators charged with excitement held movie cameras poised to record the low thunderous fly bys. The feats were phenomenal and performances mesmerizing. At one show, Mom stopped to rewind her camera and, when she looked back up, the only thing left to shoot was distant specks in the sky followed by four vapor trails.

Charles was a flight leader based on skill and experience. In Europe and Korea, he sharpened his abilities to reach senior pilot on schedule and now he commanded a squadron. Pilots of the 44th gave and got respect based on what they did, not skin color. It was ideal for Charles, an eye opener for some whites, and over all very rewarding. He was doing the important work of preparing others for the battlefront and protecting the southern perimeter which buffered the US and its allied nations from aggressors in Asia. He hated to see the assignment come to an end.

Years later, my brother Ron learned a true story which captured the genuine measure of esteem the Boys of the 44th felt toward Dad. The source was Ron Smith, a white Operations Officer stationed at Clark Field during the time Dad commanded the 44th. My brother met Smith by chance while the two men were mooring boats after a outing on Puget Sound in Seattle, Washington. In casual conversation, they discovered that both were pilots. Comparing aviation careers, a common link emerged and Ron Smith realized he was talking to Chuck

McGee's son! He went on to relate a revealing event none of us knew about prior to this fateful encounter.

During a visit to Clark Field, the wealthy father of one of the pilots of the 44th wanted to throw a big party for the squadron. Because of the father's attitude about race, the son went to him in advance, letting him know the commander of the 44th was a black man. When the father said Charles would not be invited, his son informed him if Charles was not welcome, then he would not attend and he could guarantee no pilot from the 44th would step foot in the party.

Changing his mind, the father decided he wanted to meet this man who was so well regarded by those he led.

IX: Montgomery to Minneapolis

1953-1955
- On May 17, 1954, Justice Warren delivered the unanimous Supreme Court ruling in Brown vs. The Board of Education, declaring racial segregation in schools unconstitutional.
- Following televised investigations of alleged communist subversion, the U.S. Senate voted to condemn Joe McCarthy's actions.

Charles was able to extend his tour in the Philippines six months in hopes of flying the F-86, but that didn't happen. Orders to Air Command and Staff School (ACSS) arrived for him to attend the Field Officers Course, class 53-B. Instead of looking back, he looked to the future. There were milestones he hadn't reached on the road to advancement and ACSS was one. When Charles' orders sending him there came through, it was an opportunity he accepted, even though in May of 1953 it meant moving with his family to Montgomery, Alabama.

After relocating, it didn't take long before the McGee's again faced the stark realities of highly segregated southern living, a sharp contrast to the acceptance and feeling of belonging they experienced in the Philippines. With family lodging unavailable on base the first challenge was to find housing in Montgomery. A recently widowed woman rented them a house not far from Alabama State, one of the historically black colleges. I was enrolled in third grade in the demonstration school at the college, an alternative to entering the racist public school system. No matter what precautions were taken though, a black living in Alabama could not be spared the humiliation imposed by prejudice. In the classroom, Charles studied military doctrine and philosophy; outside he and his family were learning more immediately applicable lessons in survival.

Shortly after his arrival at Maxwell Field, Charles made his first visit to the barber shop to keep his dark wavy hair in regulation military cut. He was sitting in the barber chair, chatting with the barber before the possibility dawned on the barber.

"Are you Negro?"

"Yes I am."

"Well, I can't cut your hair."

"Then let's talk with the base commander."

Quick arrangements were made for a black barber to set up a separate shop.

Even though the power of the all mighty greenback had gained blacks entry to many stores in Montgomery and Atlanta, where they sometimes traveled, the rules of a separatist society still prevailed. Frances was told she couldn't try on a hat she was admiring in one shop and, on more than one occasion, she had to snatch me and my brother away from drinking fountains labeled "Whites Only."

"We didn't like it, but we did what we had to do."

Negroes in search of restrooms were told there were no facilities, when in reality there were no facilities for them or their children. Frances' cousin, Eleanor Conrad, had passed along a solution she devised when told her small daughter couldn't use the restroom in a Dallas department store.

"CeCe, you'll have to turn up and do your business right here on the floor, since they won't let you use the bathroom!"

Mother and daughter were quickly ushered to the "nonexistent" accommodations.

Many years would pass with more than their share of close calls and harrowing experiences before an audience member asked Charles, following his presentation, what was the most difficult thing he ever had to do. I was on hand for the talk and, like the others, curiously and unsuspectingly awaited his reply.

"Trying to explain to my daughter why she couldn't play in a park one block from our house in Montgomery, Alabama. That was tougher than any military assignment. To this day I still don't know what I said to her."

These trials were part of the grooming which prepared Charles to be a leader. While they steeled his nerve and heightened his resolve, the indignities he endured outside the classroom did not outwardly affect his attitude or change his bearing.

"It kept our noses to the grindstone to see that there were still a lot of folks out there that had to be shown."

Even though he had to be careful about where to buy gasoline, how to shop and even how to walk down the street, Charles didn't carry a chip on his shoulder and thankfully, the system within ACSS dealt with him fairly. He was graded on performance, and on that basis readied for advancement. The six months of school seemed like they would never end and when time for graduation finally came, he and Frances were glad to leave the south and its restricting way of life.

The move in January, 1954, was to Minneapolis, Minnesota where, despite the freezing temperatures, things would surely be better. Upon arrival, Charles picked a large Realtor from the pages of classified ads and made an appointment to see houses. When he and Frances showed up at the office, it turned out the agent had nothing to show them despite several full pages of listings in the newspaper. The task of lodging his family was no easier in Minneapolis than in Montgomery.

In his new assignment, Charles was once more responsible for monitoring area defenses, this time in the Air Defense Control Center. For several months he covered his shift in the windowless blockhouse at Wold Chamberland Field. It was a staff job, not a command. Stateside commands were not available for black officers. Daniel "Chappie" James was the first to break through the color barrier when he was given a command at Otis Air Base outside Boston in 1956. It took the "super human" attributes he possessed to make it happen. Not only was he a proven leader, but he was good at everything he tried. Whether public speaking, sports, singing or dancing, Chappie was an all around star who could not be held down. He opened the door.

A few months after arriving in Minneapolis, the 337th FIS (Fighter Interceptor Squadron) was activated and equipped with the Northrup F-89D Scorpion, a twin engine jet aircraft. Charles was transferred to the 337th located at Ft. Snelling adjacent to the Minneapolis Airport as maintenance officer, a position he held for the next year. He moved the family into a roomy upstairs apartment in a house he found in St. Paul. Although it was not close to the base, it provided a good situation for Frances and the three children. A friend of Charles' lived not far from them and the two families enjoyed doing things together on the weekends. Saturdays often included fishing, followed by a fish fry or, depending on the catch, a big pot of chili.

One Saturday Charles came in with a nice string of fish. Enjoying a cold beer while Frances cleaned and cooked them, he was anticipating the taste of crispy pan-fried blue gill, reward for a good day's catch. The evening stretching out before them promised to be very pleasant. A typical toddler, Yvonne was into everything and her father's empty beer can looked like a shiny toy. With backs turned for a few seconds, she got her hands on it and quickly began to break out in huge red hives. The swelling spread and within minutes she was covered with them and fighting for breath. There was no time to waste. An ambulance was called and rushed her and Mom to Children's Hospital. Following by car, Dad was close behind. At the emergency room, it took extraordinary measures to save her life.

When Yvonne was stabilized, she was admitted to the hospital. Days of testing confirmed a lethal allergy to fish. The fish oil on the beer can had been enough to trigger her first attack. Had she eaten fish, rather than the more superficial exposure, the outcome may have proven fatal. The testing uncovered other allergies, milder in nature, but leading to years of allergy shots and modifications of her surroundings and activities. For Yvonne, who was barely three years old, it was the beginning of many precautions which would change her life, and ours too since we now had to protect her from natural enemies, ranging from room dust to animal hairs.

We were not immune to other dangers in our midst. Two white men had been sent by the landlord to paint our apartment. Dad, who left for the base early in the morning and didn't return until supper, had no contact with them. There was a younger painter and the other, an older man who had one eye on his painting and one on me. With Mom running an errand one afternoon, he got his chance. He caught me in the hallway, pinning me against the wall with the weight of his body, and told me if I was a good girl he could do nice things for me. Even at ten, I knew I was in danger.

Struggling free, I got away from him and found a hiding place where I stayed until Mom returned. For the rest of the afternoon I kept close to her, but didn't say a word until both men left. Very disturbed by what I told her as soon as they were gone, Mom immediately let Dad know, insisting something had to be done. Dad asked me to tell him exactly what happened and after hearing it knew this was a matter for the police. I had to repeat the whole sordid encounter again, this time explaining it to police investigators who came to the house. Dad was there, never doubting me, hesitating in his confidence we could get through the ordeal, or wavering in his commitment to see justice done. Someone with lesser conviction might have backed away, thinking there was no way the police

*would take the word a ten year old black girl accusing a white
man of molesting her.*

*With my father's encouragement I told my story to the police
and answered their questions the best I could. Dad raised us to
always tell the truth no matter how difficult, but what would
happen if the police didn't believe me or chose to do nothing
about it? The investigators took the complaint seriously. When
painters showed up the next day, the old man was not with
them. We learned he had been picked up for questioning and
ultimately arrested. Dad acted to protect his family and the
system of justice did not let us down. I was shaken by the
incident and at the same time oddly reassured. Though we
eventually closed that ugly chapter and moved on, we would be
irrevocably changed.*

Charles worked as Aircraft Maintenance Officer under a new
squadron commander, Lt. Col. James Wells. The squadron was
under considerable pressure from headquarters to have more
aircraft in commission and ready to fly. As a part of Air
Defense Command (ADC), he and the Operations Officer, Maj.
George Parker, had aircraft standing alert 24 hours a day.
Parker was likewise pressured to see that all air crew members
met a specific number of flying requirements. From Parker's
view, Charles' performance was outstanding under these
difficult circumstances.

In August of 1955, Charles moved to Central Air Defense
Headquarters at Grandview Air Base south of Kansas City,
Missouri. The new maintenance assignment was Assistant
Director of Aircraft and Missiles. Shortly after his arrival his
performance report was forwarded from Minnesota and the
endorsement by the group commander had downgraded the
report from its initial rating. The altered findings stated
maintenance and supply records were bad and too much time
had been spent on outside activities. As maintenance officer in
charge, the modified rating had the potential for significantly
damaging Charles' military career and he knew he had to

appeal. The record keeping he instituted while with the 337th would ultimately serve to refute the report and strike the downgraded rating from the record. Armed with stats, he was able to document the actual attainments point for point, including the fact that outside activities noted to as a negative were in reality flight time needed to maintain his flying status and night classes Charles took to continue progress toward a college degree.

The group commander also downgraded the report of the white operations officer, George Parker, and squadron commander, Jim Wells, who served over the same period. Like Charles, Parker kept charts to prove to higher headquarter's inspectors that it simply was not possible to comply with their requests for more unless they worked the men considerably beyond the normal eight hour day. Nevertheless his argument did not prevail. Parker and Wells were unable to have their ratings overturned. It is not clear what motivated the downgrade or prevented the reversal in the cases of the other two men. Both retired from the Air Force without further promotion.

The Parkers and the McGee's became friends in spite of Lois Parker's "southern belle" heritage. Frances found it hard to forgive her for transgressions which were remnants of her upbringing. They emerged in unexpected faux pas, like "complimenting" Yvonne by calling her a "cute little nigger baby." Dad on the other hand was more willing to allow people the opportunity to grow, learning from their mistakes, especially if he believed they were intent on changing. George spoke of Charles as "a gentleman in all respects on all occasions" saying of him "….He always had a nice smile, displayed patience-- yet, with a sense of perseverance. His mannerism...caused anyone working with him to feel that here is a man of wonderful qualities. He seemed to show with body language as well as words that he was a person of integrity, dedicated to his work, loyal and always kind.... He thus gained the respect and confidence of others easily. His family always had an appearance, which made me think that those traits I saw in Charles...(were) reflected in them. I felt he must be a good father too."

Charles had the fortitude to rise above unfairness and adversity, to focus on possibilities and move ahead with hope. On the job he was breaking new ground. Like other Tuskegee Airmen who remained in the service, in many assignments he was the first black officer to attain higher levels of authority in his unit. Being commanded by a black superior officer was a new experience and, despite the myth blacks could not lead and give orders to whites, it was working. By example, he showed the way. In Kansas City, his good name cleared, he was ready to move forward.

X: Going to Kansas City

1956-1958

● Rosa Park's refusal to give up her seat and move to the back of the bus led to her arrest and the successful year-long Montgomery bus boycott.

● Under the protection of federalized Arkansas National Guard, black teenagers enrolled in Little Rock's all-white Central High School in September, 1957.

● After withdrawal by France in 1957, conflicts erupted between the communist Vietcong and the democratic government of South Vietnam.

● Intermediate-range ballistic missiles were deployed and the U.S. launched earth satellites in 1958.

The move to Central Air Defense Force (CADF) headquarters at Grandview Air Force Base offered Charles an opportunity for greater responsibilities at a higher level within the military hierarchy. In 1956 the Korean War was winding to a close and with Russia's move into eastern Europe, the cold war was heating up. CADF was at the heart of activity in the region and Charles was on the team responsible for the readiness of forces.

Missiles were the primary air defense ordinance. They included a mix of guidance systems and fusings: contact missiles, heat seeking missiles and others adapted to various purposes. Like aircraft, missiles required ongoing ground support to assure mission effectiveness. The ability to respond had to be tested on a regular basis. Headquarters conducted these tests and part of Charles' work was support for the inspector's office.

Field inspections could be focused on a specific squadron or broad and encompassing, affecting an entire command. Sometimes they were announced and at others unexpected ("no notice"). A message sent from central command post notified unit command posts of change in the defense posture. In the case of a national emergency, the word would come from Washington to all units. The first level of response was "alert." Unless on official leave of absence, military personnel were on duty 24 hours a day and leave could be canceled at a moment's notice. All servicemen had to have a way to be contacted.

A raise to the second level, "stand by," meant equipment had to be moved into position. If conditions worsened, the third level called for "deployment." This was the response system Charles tested, measuring the strengths and weaknesses of units in the command. Where the response was insufficient an analysis would determine if the cause was equipment, supplies or staff.

As the saying went, "I'm the inspector and I'm here to help you, (with a sharp pencil in hand)."

Not long after being at Headquarters, Charles heard rumor he would be promoted to Lieutenant Colonel. The assignment to headquarters in a position calling for a higher rank enhanced his prospects and contributed to the recommendation. When promotions were being processed, "word" usually got out before formal notification. With official notification came the traditional office party, cigars passed out and folks stopping by to offer congratulations. Later, there was the pinning of the silver oak leaf clusters which was almost anticlimactic when the time finally arrived.

Away from work, Charles and his family were settling in the first home of their own, a bungalow on 52nd Street in Kansas City, Missouri. There were several towns closer to Grandview Air Base, Grandview, Belton and Hickman Mills, but a black family couldn't even park a trailer in these communities. The house was fourteen miles from base and, with single lane highways, about a thirty-five minute drive in normal traffic. The trip could be made in less time, but undue haste might result in a traffic ticket which, like a bounced check, was not good on the military record.

It was the first year for school desegregation in Kansas City. The local school board had responded to the Brown vs. The Board of Education decision by the Supreme Court, the ruling prompted by a case originating in the neighboring state of Kansas.

52nd street was the northern boundary of a pocket community of black families. Blacks lived between 52nd and 55th and between Prospect and Bellefountain. The relatively new, all brick Graceland Elementary School was right across the street from us. Ron and I and the other black children in that area would attend Graceland along with white children from the other side of the invisible divide. Had the McGee's moved to Kansas City the year before, we would have attended the black school which was housed in a wooden building with a pot belly stove on the corner of 55th and South Benton.

Neither Ron nor I experienced any particular incidents or unrest associated with school integration in Kansas City. Our easy entry was due in part to the military experience on base where youngsters of different races were more accustomed to going to school and playing together.

Although most things were going well, I remembered my first real fight happened at Graceland. A tough white girl took a serious disliking to me. She was a creep and a bully and from her point of view, I guess I was a little too smart for my own good. When the challenge was issued, I decided I had to face her. With clenched fists, a knot in the pit of my stomach and staunch determination, I walked back to the school yard at the appointed time. She was there. We exchanged blows and rolled around long enough to call it a draw, while one of her sidekicks looked on, but fortunately did not join the fray. I remember feeling something important had been decided that day. I walked a little taller as I headed home, preparing to explain my disheveled appearance to my mother. Something told me Dad would understand.

In my naiveté, I didn't see race as a factor in the dispute. From my vantage, ignorance motivated that girl. In hindsight, I imagine it was both. Two things became evident in the aftermath. One, I would not back down from a fight. The other, I would not automatically see individual differences as racially motivated. Without my conscious knowledge, guiding principles were being passed from one generation to the next.

Much of our life on 52nd Street was tranquil. The Lewis' lived two doors away (and they would become our life long friends). Their son, Ronald, and my brother were the same age and soon became inseparable. We met the Giles and their daughters and son who lived on the opposite corner. Phyllis was a little older than me. She taught me great childhood sayings like, "the blacker the berry the sweeter the juice, except when they're black as you, they ain't got no juice." That began Mom and Dad's crusade to stamp the word ain't from my vocabulary. Phyllis also taught me that black people could dislike me too, especially if they thought I had advantages they didn't. The Dudleys and daughter, Anita, my first remembered girlfriend, lived a half block down the hill on South Benton. As far as I could tell, Anita was enjoying each day and looking forward to the future with no time for resentment.

We owned a tree covered lot adjoining the house. A part of the block behind was undeveloped woods, great for exploring. After music lessons, dinner and homework, we were allowed to roam our domain until the street lights came on. It was a time of freedom and adventure. Many summer hours were spent laying in the grass, peering up through the trees to watch clouds roll by overhead. In the evenings, fire flies filled the air and we filled our glass jars, using an ice pick to make holes in the metal lids. We learned to pinch their lighted tails to make rings and debated if it was a bad thing to do. Dad advised us to release the "lightning" bugs so they wouldn't die and, even though we liked the light show, we ultimately decided it was better to let them go at the end of the day.

In Kansas City, Charles and his family became active in the Christian Church (Disciples of Christ). Military services had been mainly ecumenical, since there were so many different faiths to be considered. Charles grew up in the A.M.E. church and Frances was a Baptist. When they thought the time had come for their children to make a church decision, they visited several churches in the area, finally settling on West Paseo Christian Church at 2454 West Paseo Boulevard.

For Charles, spirituality was as much a part of his life as patriotism. He believed in a divine creator and in living by the Lord's precepts, and wanted that source of strength and assurance for his children. The West Paseo Christian Church had the message, the music and the decorum he and Frances looked for in worship services. Charles' baptism in the A.M.E. church had been the standard sprinkling. In the tradition of the Christian church, he was baptized by submersion. He also joined the choir, agreeing to add the scarce commodity of a tenor voice.

The routine of our family on Sundays centered around church. Sunday mornings were always a rush to get everyone up, dressed, fed and out the door on time for the twenty minute ride to church. Often the pace left the atmosphere for the first part of the car ride a bit strained and less than charitable, but by the time we arrived, tempers had calmed and civility returned. When the choir marched in, I was filled with the Christian spirit befitting worship services. Rev. S. S. Myers had a booming voice and compelling message and he and his family were inspiring role models. At West Paseo, we were surrounded by good people and strong families. I saw my Dad as a leader among them, whether solemnly marching in a regal choir robe, speaking words of welcome or sympathy at the podium or jovially shaking hands in the lobby after services. He was a key figure in the life of the church, always giving freely of his time and talent for the benefit of its congregation.

Charles was similarly charitable in other areas of his life. He continued district committee work he had begun with Boy Scouts of American in Minnesota, where he served as district director for the Great Plains Region, receiving the Silver Beaver Award for his work. He also joined Beta Lambda, the alumni chapter of the Alpha Phi Alpha Fraternity. The Alphas were active socially and civically. Their programs were designed to motivate young people toward achievement and excellence in education. The importance of education was one of the hallmarks of Alpha programs and consistent with Charles' personal values. He served the Alphas in a number of capacities, including a rotation through the officer positions and stint as President of the Chapter.

The Alphas were strong advocates of family within the brotherhood and beyond. They sponsored great picnics and the grandest parties which usually made the society page of the black newspaper, The Kansas City Call. For picnics, everyone got together at nearby Swope Park or Lake Jacomo. Families piled into station wagons and sedans along with dishes of potato salad, baked beans, deviled eggs, cobblers and cakes. Unloading on the other end, portable games were distributed and sports equipment set up. Frances and the other woman coordinated the food and looked after the babies and toddlers. The men manned the grills for hours, basting barbecued spare ribs, and flipping hamburgers. They stocked coolers (and emptied them), while setting up nets, pacing off ball diamonds and making sure the meat didn't burn too badly. Those of us too young to be of much help, ran off to explore the territory and occupy ourselves teasing, flirting and playing until it was time to eat.

These days were happy and relatively carefree, filled with fun and fellowship. Whether fishing, playing baseball, or lounging in the shade, the day went by too quickly. Parents recognized the signs of exhaustion setting in, but kids were still reluctant to say good-by and had to be coaxed into autos for the evening drive home. The Clarence Robinsons, Eugene Petersons, Carl Petersons...folks in the extended family who shared these memorable outings.

Alpha parties, a social highlight, were for adults only. My sister, brother and I watched as Mom and Dad transformed themselves into fashion models prepared for an elegant night on the town. They sparkled like movie stars as they gave last minute instructions to the baby sitter and kissed entranced offspring before stepping out arm and arm to dance the night away. Their glamour ignited our young psyches and visions of the ball filled our heads as the sandman finally claimed us on those enchanted evenings.

Interspersed in Charles' busy schedule were enjoyable, but all too infrequent golf outings with Harold Holiday, Leroy Lewis, Carl Peterson and other friends and associates. The Kansas City years had their scary and sad moments too. We got news that Lewis Jr. died unexpectedly. He had been living as somewhat a recluse in northern Illinois and apparently succumbed to a brain hemorrhage while in his home, his body not immediately discovered. Although the brothers had been out of touch, Lewis Jr.'s death was a shock that ended any hope of rekindling the closeness they had once known. I had never seen my Dad more somber than on the trip to attend my uncle's funeral. Uncle Lewis' lifeless body was the first one I remember seeing. It caused me to seriously contemplate death for a time and I worried about it awhile after. Though Dad was sad, neither he nor Mom seemed to fear death and they reassured me when I crept into their room after losing the nightly battle with my fears. They were patient and comforting and always managed to convince me to go back to bed so all of us could get some sleep.

Not longafter, Mom had to have surgery. Her kidney was removed after a massive calcium deposit was discovered blocking the kidney ducts. Her mother, Momma Nellie, came to take care of us while Mom was recuperating. During the months Momma Nellie was there, we learned that good health can not be taken for granted and old people can be crotchety, especially if rubber balls bounced too close to them. Somehow we all managed to get through it.

As Mom regained strength, she treated herself to the "works" at her favorite beauty shop. After investing hours she returned home in full make up with coal-black hair arranged in the latest fancy hairdo, and bright red lips and nails. I was still trying to form an opinion about this new image when Yvonne took one look, burst into tears, and became inconsolable. The new look was far too racy for Momma Nellie's taste and drew a puzzled "what's the big deal" glance from Ron. I don't think Dad even saw the full effect of his wife's transformation, because within the hour Mom emerged from the bathroom without makeup and with her hair returned to its normal style. Yvonne was greatly relieved to have her mother back.

When I started eighth grade at Paseo High School, most of the black kids met at 54th street each morning for the twenty five minute walk to school. It never occurred to me I wouldn't be allowed to join them. I was crushed when Dad divulged this fact. He patiently explained it made no sense for me to go two blocks out of my way to join the group. No matter how I begged and pleaded, he would not change his mind. Crying well into the night, I had red, swollen eyes when Anita (whose parents were similarly practical) and I started our trek from 52nd Street on the first day. In hindsight, the lesson I learned was no matter how difficult it seemed or how bad it felt at the time, it didn't kill me to be different or separate from the crowd. Decisions should be made based on reason, not on what everyone else is doing.

With work, school, church, social activities and family life, the time in Kansas City came and went. In the service, tours of duty sometimes lasted three years, but rarely much longer.

After that you expected to move on. News came that Charles would be assigned to the Pentagon. Closeness to the seat of power might seem like a plus, and while true in many cases, the Pentagon was the exception for him. In 1958, it was not necessarily a stepping stone for a Major or Lieutenant Colonel.

"(At the Pentagon) you are lost in a great big shuffle with lots of stars (general officers) and eagles (full Colonels) around taking credit, while you're doing the work."

That's the way Charles saw it, but again he didn't try to get the assignment changed. Shortly afterward, the official orders were delivered. Instead of the Pentagon, they were to send Charles on an unaccompanied tour to an unknown location; the family would not be able to join him. For overseas assignments the Air Force used Army Post Office (APO) numbers. This assignment was to APO unknown, with instructions to report to headquarters of U.S. Air Forces Europe in Wiesbaden, Germany.

XI: Tour in Europe

1959-1962

- Alaska and Hawaii became states in 1959.
- In the 1960s, intercontinental ballistic missiles joined the arsenal of weapons used to wage the Cold War with the Soviet Union.
- Sit-in protests, begun at a lunch counter in Greensboro, North Carolina, spread across the country.
- In January of 1961 John F. Kennedy became the country's youngest President.
- Groups of black and white Freedom Riders took bus trips from Washington D.C. through the South to challenge segregation.
- Late in 1961 the U.S. began sending U.S. Air Force and Army personnel to South Vietnam to train and advise its armed forces.

Charles was one of a cadre of officers assigned to the 7230th Support Squadron. The unknown aspect of his orders stemmed from United States negotiations with Italy and Turkey to locate Jupiter missiles, the newest weapon in the U.S. arsenal being deployed to counter the Cold War threat. Recalling the history of the time, the Italian government was unstable. Battling factions were in power only a few months before a no confidence vote resulted in a change of power, slowing the progress of negotiations.

In January of 1959, Charles and the others assigned to the 7230th were delayed in Germany on a temporary duty assignment. After weeks of this undesirable arrangement with no end in sight to the negotiation, orders appeared saying the group had been given a permanent change of station (PCS) to US Air Forces Europe (USAFE). This may have gone unchallenged accept it was a PCS excluding families. The men registered their complaint saying that a PCS without families was unfair. Reluctantly, the Air Force agreed. It was June before travel could be arranged and late summer before families arrived overseas.

The months we spent in Kansas City after Dad left stand out as a defining period, at first somewhat scary. With the exception of short temporary duty assignments, we weren't used to Dad not being with us, especially at night. Concerned for our safety, my mind conjured up bad guys who would find out Dad was away and seize the opportunity to overpower the "women and children" for some evil purpose. I was constantly on the look out for suspicious people or suspect behavior and not alone in my worries. Nerves became frayed and tempers flared. There were more fights at the dinner table and the pressures of single parenting took their toll on Mom.

As time passed, we learned to cope in this less than desirable circumstance and I sensed us rising to the occasion. Mom handled things that, as far as I knew, she never had to deal with before, and I helped. Dad had talked with me in advance about Mom needing my support and I began to understand what he meant and what he expected of me.

Mom's birthday was January 27th and before leaving, Dad entrusted me with a gift she wasn't to know about. I took the charge seriously and hid it where I hoped she wouldn't find it. As the day approached, Mom kept her eye on the mail and I saw her disappointment when nothing arrived. The evening of 27th Ron, Yvonne and I arranged a surprise party for the four of us, complete with cake, candles, a few small gifts and the special prize, a gift from Dad.

I never forgot how happy we made her that night. Until the last minute, we acted like we didn't even know it was her birthday. Just when she thought she had been forgotten, we sprung the surprise. She was instantly full of smiles, hugs and tears of joy. After the excitement died down, she asked how we pulled it off. As I told her the details, I saw her looking at me with new appreciation. It felt great, like I'd grown up a lot all at once. The gift from Dad also let us know he was with us, even though he couldn't be there in person. Afterward we had newfound confidence and worked together more as a team.

By the time we received orders and were prepared to go to Germany, Dad's situation had changed again. The 7230th cadre would be going to Italy after all. The governments finally reached an agreement and Louigi Balogna Sea Plane Base in Taranto, Italy, was chosen as the location for the American missile support contingent. The men were studying German in night classes, but quickly switched to Italian, a tough transition since there was so much difference in pronunciation. While we were traveling to Wiesbaden, Germany, Dad was heading to Taranto, Italy.

In 1959, the exam Charles took back in 1947 finally caught up with him when he got a letter appointing him to a regular commission. A colonel in the Reserve, he was enjoying flying so much that he accepted the regular USAF rank of lieutenant colonel and went to Italy to deploy the Jupiter missile. The 7230th was responsible for supporting the American civilian and military technicians coming from Red Stone Arsenal in Alabama. The missiles were deployed around Gioia del Colle Air Base, but ownership and control of the warheads was retained by the Americans, supported from the sea plane base at Taranto. In preparation for the squadron, buildings were converted to establish a small exchange (store), commissary, chapel and school. The motor pool and other support services were provided by the Italians. Headquarters and classrooms for the grade school shared one building and a mess hall, supply area and the exchange were located at the lower level of the compound. Club facilities were a half hour ride away from base in a breathtakingly beautiful setting on the Ionian Sea.

Charles was Deputy Commander of the cadre, but within the year he assumed command when Colonel Summers was transferred. In the meantime, Frances arrived and established the children in Germany where they started school. We lived in Alcum, a housing area on the German economy (off base), and took a bus to school on base. Now accustomed to fending for ourselves, we made the transition smoothly. As one of a few pilots in the support squadron, Charles flew the C-47 cargo plane back and forth carrying supplies between Italy and Germany, so we saw him fairly often.

There was no American high school in Taranto, so when the time came to move the family to Italy, I stayed behind. Not yet fourteen, I was ambivalent about the prospects of living in the student dormitory in Germany, separated from my family thousands of miles away. Dad pointed out that I wouldn't really be alone. There were other kids, whose parents were stationed in Taranto, living in the dorm. As often as possible, he would come to see me and I would be able to come to Taranto for the summers and school breaks. If he harbored any doubts about the situation, he didn't show them. Mom's anxiety, on the other hand, was written all over her face when we said our good-byes. As hard as it was, military life had prepared us for this. We did what we had to and made the best of it.

At Gioia del Colle, Charles had his first base command. His prior command experience was at squadron level. Here the entire responsibility rested with him. As base commander, he had a car and driver. The car was a dark sedan, easily recognizable with an Italian flag displayed on one front fender and an American flag on the other. The nature of the mission in Taranto was classified, giving the operation an air of mystery and intrigue. In reality, much of Charles' activity related less to the presence of the Jupiter missiles and more to the formalities and requirements of operating an American enclave on foreign soil.

As base commander, Charles was the official representative to the Italian government and involved in many interactions ranging from routine matters to troubleshooting when problems arose. Interpersonal conflicts inevitably emerged when the two cultures came together. Some Italians were opposed in principle to the American presence and others became less accepting based on unpleasant experiences, but many were genuinely cooperative and hospitable. All were curious about the American visitors in their midst. Italians in the military and local municipal governing structure transacted business with Charles and soon learned he was an effective leader and man of principle. They found him to be a respectful guest in their land with an important military job to do, and he balanced the roles beautifully. The "Coronello," as they called him, was not only invited to their offices, but he and his family were welcomed into their homes as well.

Frances adapted well to life in Italy. She made friends with American and Italian families. Most relationships were cordial, if not genuinely warm and friendly.

There was one notable exception. She took a distinct dislike to an attractive Italian woman who Charles had dinner with one night while Frances and the children were still in Germany. She was a single woman from town employed on base. Apparently, the dinner with Dad was enough to put her on Mom's "persona non grata" list and no matter how solicitous the woman was, Frances never said a kind word to her.

The Americans under Charles' charge depended heavily on him. He listened to their concerns and refereed disputes, including the controversial issue of whether or not sex education would be taught in the base school. Not much teaching material on the subject was available in the dependent school system and working with the school administrator, a physician and representatives of the clergy, he ultimately approved a curriculum presented by Barbara Peter, one of the dependent wives who was a registered nurse. There was only one girl whose parents would not allow her to attend the class. This was one of many things he dealt with which were not taught in staff school. Without a blueprint, Charles relied on honesty, compassion, fairness and mutual respect to achieve results. Under his leadership the servicemen and their families at Taranto formed close ties and attachments that remained strong for decades.

Not all Americans were well thought of in Taranto. Some came with a different attitude and clashed with the local populace. They brought a belief in American superiority and acted out their prejudices. There were some who forbade their teenage daughters to dance with Italian boys or allowed their younger children to spit and throw water balloons from apartment balconies. Their behavior amounted to a first hand performance of the "Ugly American," which was embarrassing and shameful. Charles worked to combat prejudices and enlighten these emissaries of intolerance. Results were mixed. Ultimately, he supported one landlord's decision to evict all but three American families and would not intercede any further on behalf of those ousted.

Taranto dependents in school in Germany had been instructed not to talk about the base in Italy. This restriction led to a few awkward instances whenever I was reluctant to say where home was. These were short-lived, however, because within moments, other students would smile knowingly and say," Oh, your Dad must be with the secret missile base in southern Italy."

The good soldier follows orders and I only smiled back in response.

True to his word, Dad came to visit me in Wiesbaden a number of times. The excitement would build before his arrival and, when the day finally came, I dressed up for the occasion because we usually went to a fancy restaurant at the Von Stueben or American Arms hotel or sometimes a party. We would dine on steak and lobster as he showed me how to select the right wine and test it. German Reislings from the Mosel

River area were among his favorites. I felt grown up and very elegant when we went out on these special evenings.

On one trip, he took me to the home of a German woman named Anita. He worked with her when he first came to Germany and we were invited to join her, her brother and parents for a holiday celebration. The food was delicious and the drink flowed freely. The festive atmosphere was embellished by the cherry punch loaded with alcohol. As the evening wore on, I noticed Anita glancing at Dad. She was undoubtedly infatuated with him, which was obvious even to my adolescent eyes. I didn't hold it against her because, in truth, it would be hard for her not to be taken with this handsome, considerate American officer.

Since I was more than a little tipsy by the end of the evening, getting me back to the dorm was a bit tricky. Fortunately the lobby was empty when we arrived with me wrapped in streamers, sprinkled with confetti and smiling ear to ear. Dad stood me up straight, pointed me toward the stairs and said, "Walk directly to your room and get into bed. I'll call you in the morning."

I followed his orders to the letter.

My first visit to Taranto was impressive. Dad flew a C-47 to Germany to pick up supplies and high school students heading home for Christmas break. There were seven or eight of us and we all donned parachutes and Mae West life preservers which we wore for the duration of the ten hour flight. There was no bathroom on board, although the males had the luxury of being able to relieve themselves through a tube in the side of the plane. There were no cushioned seats either, nor was there insulation, so the trip was a real test of endurance. I walked to the cockpit to talk with Dad from time to time to break the monotony. He assigned me the task of keeping an eye on one of the gauges. It never moved much and I finally lost interest, later deciding it had been his way of keeping me from being too much of a pest.

Italy was magnificent. After the excitement of warm reunions at the airport, Dad entered his car and was whisked away to headquarters, while Mom, Ron and Yvonne took me into the city to our apartment along the waterfront. It was on the third floor of a new high rise known as the Pink Palace. The halls of the apartment were wide and expansive and all the floors were marble. The balcony which crossed the front of the living room overlooked the sea and the view was spectacular. Even the bedrooms had balconies. I had never lived any place quite so luxurious.

As the base commander's family, we were recognized everywhere we went. For the first time I was conscious of being "the Colonel's daughter." Exploring town, I could get away from that distinction, but as a young black woman on the streets of Taranto, I was a curiosity and drew attention. Quickly, I learned the interest was not malicious and continued to enjoy exploring. The times I enjoyed most were nights on the balcony watching the lights of the fishing boats as they returned to the harbor, and days on silver beaches by the turquoise sea. These scintillating afternoons on the shore were followed by dinner at the nearby Officer's Club, where those in attendance were always delighted to see the Colonel and his family. The meals were sumptuous and service impeccable with the staff catering to our every wish.

No doubt this was an idyllic view of Taranto. While some Italians in the area were well off, particularly those we came into contact with, the local economy was impoverished by U.S. standards. The people, on the other hand, had a warm and generous nature and joy for living, making them content beyond most Americans. The experience and Dad's handling of it put our relative affluence in perspective. Fullness of life was not measured by material possessions.

Too soon, each summer or holiday stay ended and Dad loaded up the students and flew us back to school.

In 1961, American high school students from Taranto were transferred to the school in Dreux, France, thirty miles outside Paris. There I completed my junior year with the kids from Taranto and American dependents from other military stations, including the not yet famous Priscilla Presley. It was there, Driscoll, a white boy born and bred in the deep American South, told me I was different than he expected a black person to be. It was there several girls, claiming to have my best interest at heart, told me I was getting "to close" to Rudy, a white classmate. They suggested for the good of all we remain just friends.

As it had been for Dad, high school was a time for learning about discrimination and prejudice. Like him, I was hurt by bias and mistreatment, but didn't let these incidents affect my outward demeanor. Like him, I kept these feelings to myself while striving to make a difference.

During the year in France, I decided to smoke cigarettes, which required parental permission. On one of his trips north, I asked Dad about it and he told me to weigh the pros and cons and let him know what I thought when he returned.

On his next visit I had permission slip in hand and wanted him to sign it.

"Wrong decision," he said, a steady gaze leveled at me.

I was shocked and protested.

"If you weren't going to let me smoke, why didn't you just say so?"

"I wanted you to think about it very carefully, but I never said I would agree."

This was a man who would give me the latitude to be an independent thinker, but not enough rope to hang myself. While

I sneaked a cigarette or two, for the most part I abided by his wishes because I believed he had my best interests at heart.

That was harder to believe when the magical years in Italy drew to a close and he told me we would be moving to Minot, North Dakota, in the summer of 1962.

After two years commanding the 7230th Support Squadron at Gioia del Colle, Charles with his family headed back to the USA and *(why not)* Minot, North Dakota.

XII: Great Sky Country

1962-1963

- In 1962 U.S. Air Force veteran James H. Meredith enrolled at the University of Mississippi over objections of state governor Ross Barnett.
- The Cuban missile crisis culminated in the removal of Soviet intermediate-range missile bases from Cuba in the fall of 1962.
- On June 12, 1963, NAACP leader Medgar Evers was murdered as he entered his home in Jackson, Mississippi.

Charles always seemed oblivious to his good looks. Like his race, they were a whim of fate and parentage outside his control. Top physical conditioning added to them, but resulted from discipline rather than ego. A love for sweets had the potential to add more weight than his frame could easily carry, but the standards for military pilots were strict and adherence was required. A few brushes with flying disqualification provided motivation to keep the problem in check. He adopted a routine, incorporating the Canadian 5BX program of sit ups, jumping jacks and push ups, and worked out daily.

I can't say when I first noticed his appearance. I was too close to see and other things about him being my Dad seemed more important, like whether he would let me go out on the weekend or have the car when I wanted it. Other people were not so blind or preoccupied though and eventually I began to notice them noticing him.

By the time I was in high school in 1959, Dad's wavy hair had a touch of silver gray at the temples which served to further distinguish him, especially when he was in uniform. His skin had a tanned glow and his warm brown eyes crinkled slightly when he broke into a broad smile, which he was prone to do when greeting my friends. Outward appearance and a pleasing demeanor combined to give him the distinct ability to make people glad to be in his presence.

Appreciation of his good looks crossed the boundaries of age and race. Some of the earliest comments came from school friends.

"Was that your Dad? Wow, he is really good looking!"

As the saying goes, I wish I had a nickel for every time I heard that. Thirty- five years later I was still hearing it.

"I can't believe that was your Dad. He looks great!"

"Yeah! Me either. And wearing (Bermuda) shorts! How old did you say he was?"

Same song, millionth verse. At seventy-six his legs were still muscular and shapely and he was as handsome as ever. I had come to know that with his unassuming charm and easy manner, Dad made an impression on people. It was like watching the pied piper of charisma. He piqued their interest and commanded attention initially, and within moments he was accorded their admiration.

By example, the McGee children learned how they looked was less important than what they did. While the first may gain immediate notice, it was the lasting impression that counted.

The years in Europe between 1959 and 1962 were full of drama and adventure. Vacations in Paris, Rome, Naples, Venice, and Athens, Greece opened an incredible window on the world. Charles wanted these cultural experiences for his family and he made them educational and fun. My junior year in high school, the Prom was held on the second level of the Eiffel Tower. It was the stuff movies were made of and we were living it.

Magical as they were, these years would not go on forever and the reality was the tour in Europe was coming to an end. It was time to change focus and there were important things going on in the U.S. In sharp contrast to the acceptance the McGee's experienced overseas, blacks in the States were fighting for equal access and opportunity. The civil rights movement was gaining momentum. Enough information was reaching Europe to let us know we were missing something of serious consequence.

My imagination turned to things I envisioned back home. Vivid images were conjured of cities vibrating with action from coast to coast with places like Chicago, St. Louis, and Kansas City flourishing in the heartland. Any of these locations were exciting possibilities for the next assignment. When word came, it was a blow. Minot, North Dakota! None of us had ever heard of it. A look at the atlas was not reassuring. In addition to disqualifying as a big city, Minot was in the middle of no-where. The closest landmark was the U.S. and Canadian border and there wasn't anything remotely metropolitan on either side.

In the midst of disappointment, I realized maybe I didn't have to go to North Dakota. After all, I had been away from home for three years. In one more year, I would be off to college. What difference would it make if I continued to live apart from the family after we were back in the States? With renewed enthusiasm, I approached Dad about the idea of living with my cousin Cassandra (Leonard and Stella's daughter and only child) in St. Louis. Cassie and I were less than a year apart and it made perfect sense; it was the ideal solution.

Not to Dad! What made sense to him was for the family to be together. Separation was one thing when we had no choice, but there was a high school in Minot and no amount of argument would get him to see things differently.

We flew into McGuire Air Force Base on a hot day in the summer of 1962 and took a bus to New York City where we spent the night. Not just skyscrapers, but everything in the "Big Apple" seemed oversized. A distinguished looking man passed us in a Lincoln so long I thought it must be a limousine. Compared to Italy everything was also very expensive. One day of sightseeing was enough to take in the mandatory Statue of Liberty and Empire State Building and produce sticker shock, which let Dad know we needed to move on quickly. The next morning, Mom and Dad left to pick up our car which had been shipped to a dock in New Jersey. Our instructions were simple.

"Stay in your room. Don't move, don't call (room service), don't do anything."

The following day we packed and headed inland. The ride gave us time to take in the novelties of the U.S. countryside. In Champaign, Illinois, we were reunited with extended family we hadn't seen in three years. I will never forget two unrelated events which happened in Champaign that summer. The first was a stroke of fortune; I met William, who would one day be my spouse. Second, I ran away from home over a question of integrity.

There was a puppy at Momma Nellie's house that was restricted to the back porch while being house broken. The dog got inside and made a mess at a time Dad thought I was the only one home who could have let him in. When I denied doing it, a heated exchange ensued. Dad took my insistence as insolence and slapped me! I was stunned! And hurt. More by being called a liar than the stinging cheek. It was the first time Dad had ever slapped me, plus I hadn't had a childhood whippin' in years! I was sixteen and too old for this! I decided I had to get away.

Fueled by anger, and against my better judgment, I took a hundred dollars from Mom's purse and a few belongings before sneaking out of the house. As I walked toward town a plan took shape and I went to the train station, purchasing a ticket to Chicago, convinced that Aunt Sadie would take me in. The bonus was I wouldn't have to go to North Dakota.

Before the scheduled departure, I had time to buy stationary and a stamp at the nearby dime store and mailed all but ten dollars of the remaining money to Mom. The police greeted me in front of the station as I returned to catch the train. My attempt to run away ended before I got out of town. Secretly, I was relieved. Back at home, Dad told me he found out Aunt Stella let the dog in the house. I was vindicated. Dad taught me to tell the truth and I had learned the lesson well. So well, in fact, any doubt about my honesty was a personal affront I couldn't abide. Especially from him.

From Champaign, we headed north on the final leg of the road trip which would take us to Minot. As we traveled the landmarks became fewer and farther between. The country of the big horizon lay ahead. Towns became crossroads with a gas station, store and house or two. There was not even a promised ice cream cone to be had. Rest stops were reduced to an unplumbed toilet and picnic bench and finally, a sign along the road and single trash can. We were passing through the wilderness known as the "Bad Lands," and with nothing on the horizon, it was truly "great sky" country.

Charles reported for duty as Director of Plans and Programs for the Minot Air Defense Sector. From the "Block House" he and his staff administered plans for activity in the sector, coordinating elements of air defense against the threat of Russian bombers and missiles seeking to strike over the northern border.

Deteriorating relations between Cuba and the U.S. reached a critical stage in the fall of 1962. Despite repeated denials by the Soviet Union and the Cuban government, the United States charged the Soviet Union with the establishment of intermediate-range missiles bases in Cuba, a development the United States would not tolerate since it placed significant offensive military capabilities in the Caribbean. Although the focus of preparedness was in another sector, the increased level of alert was felt as far north as Minot.

Even as crises rose around the globe, some aspects of military life were carried out in a contrasting state of normalcy.

While waiting for base housing, the McGee family occupied a small ranch house on the west side of town.

As in Italy, we were somewhat of a novelty in Minot. There was no indigenous black population. In fact, outside military personnel and their families the only other black person I saw was a cowboy who came through town with the rodeo. I distinctly remember being told, other than Mom and me, the only black women living in town were prostitutes who were imported to appease the airmen on base. (Yvonne was too young at the time to be considered a woman.)

When it came to socializing, interracial dating was taboo. Rather than miss high school milestones like the senior prom, blacks were creative in using their network of fellow officers to fill the void when suitable escorts were not available. Since I was the only black in the high school in Minot, I was in need of this service. Lieutenant Colonel John Suggs, a Tuskegee Airmen and family friend, lived two states away in Glasgow, Montana, with his wife and two sons. The families collaborated on a solution to the prom dilemma, and exported John Jr. from Glasgow to take me to my senior prom. When it was my turn to come to his rescue, I boarded a train for the 12 hour ride across "Big Sky" territory to return the favor. It is amazing the lengths our parents went to so we could have a "normal" social experience.

News bulletins were full of racial discord heating up in the cities and we were sensitive to the situation even in an isolated place like Minot. I was pretty much a loner that year, more out of resentment over the misfortune of being there than any overt show of prejudice in the local community. One day I decided not to go into a drug store prominently displaying a sign saying "We serve Whites Ice Cream," only to learn to Mom and Dad's amusement, that Whites was a brand name of the product being advertised.

Ron owned a prized jacket with Dad's squadron "Flying Devils" insignia. It was stolen from his locker at school and

Dad remembered the staff being less than helpful in their efforts to recover it. Yvonne was spit on by a kid on the playground, and a tussle ensued, resulting in a trip to the principal's office. The kid apologized. Dad and the family were glad to move on base when housing was available.

I did many things to pass the time that year I might not have otherwise done like joining Thespians, playing a role in the musical Oklahoma, and singing with a madrigal group. Practicing what I learned from Dad, I made the most of a less than desirable situation and he kept the family together.

In the year following the Cuban Missile Crisis, the Air Force reevaluated its air defense posture. The perceived threat from the Soviet Union was more remote and some military bases were deemed surplus. Minot programs were among them. Its air defense operations were to be phased out or transferred to other sectors, so after one year Charles prepared to move on. His orders called for him to go to 10th Air Force Headquarters at Richards-Gebaur Air Base, formerly Grandview AFB, near Kansas City. It would be his second tour of duty there.

I was so glad to get the news, I didn't even want to stay in Minot for high school graduation. Dad wouldn't hear of it. In June of 1963, Charles E. McGee's namesake crossed the stage of Minot Senior High School and received her diploma with classmates she barely knew, most of whom had been together since kindergarten. Such long term and close knit relationships outside immediate family were hard to imagine for a "military brat." In all fairness, other students had never been hostile; only self absorbed as most high schoolers are. My education took place in many locales over twelve years with a changing cast of friends and acquaintances, mirroring Dad's experience as the McGee family moved about in the late 1920's and 1930's.

There was only one difference of opinion between Dad and me which stood out during the year in Minot. It had to do with my evolving beliefs about interracial dating. A white airman, overlooking the barriers of rank and race, asked Dad if he could take me out. Dad gave permission. Although we talked on the phone, and he came by the house on several occasions, I never went out with him. After this had gone on for a while, Dad told me he thought it was a mistake to make a decision about dating based on race. In doing that, I would be following judgment no better than bigoted whites. I gave this matter serious thought. In the end I did not change my mind. With so many black airmen on base and only one young black woman, prostitutes aside, it didn't seem right for me to date a white man. In this case, racial sensitivity overrode concerns about racial bias. If Dad was disappointed, he never pressed the issue.

Interracial relationships remain a source of consternation and controversy. Many blacks and whites prefer to date and marry within their own race and believe everyone should adhere to their standards. Others view affairs of the heart as colorblind. The McGee's are a "rainbow" family with both views evident.

Dad did not judge the worth of individuals based on the color of their skin. Nevertheless, he distinguished racial pride from racial prejudice. Pride recognizes our African American heritage as a rich and compelling legacy to honor and preserve, but a positive self image does not demand bigotry or intolerance associated with prejudice. Diminishing others is not a prerequisite.

Dad helped me understand these feelings and put them in perspective.

A significant sign that times were changing was Charles' assignment to 10th Air Force Headquarters at Richards-Gebaur AFB based on the strength of his credentials and prior experience.

XIII: Survival Training

1963-1967

- On August 28, 1963, a quarter of a million people, led by Dr. Martin Luther King, Jr., attended the March on Washington, D.C. urging support for pending civil rights legislation.
- In October four black children were killed in a church bombing in Birmingham, Alabama.
- President John F. Kennedy was assassinated in Dallas, Texas, on November 22, 1963.
- President Lyndon B. Johnson signed the Civil Rights Act of 1964 and the Voting Rights Act of 1965.
- The U.S. began full-scale military operations in support of South Vietnam.

In the summer of 1963, it was good to be heading to Kansas City again. During the drive from Minot, we were delighted when trees reappeared on the landscape as we crossed the state boundary into Minnesota. Though we lived on base and were received more openly than the time before, we were also reunited with friends and church members in the black community fondly remembered from the previous stint in Kansas City. We moved into a comfortable ranch house on Bong Avenue and to Dad's feigned surprise admitted we had no idea Bong was a World War II pilot famed for aerial exploits, who was killed in a test flight accident. Frankly, Richards and Gebaur were also mysteries to us, but we learned they were natives of Kansas City who were killed in the line of duty during the first and second World Wars. I stayed in Kansas City long enough to help Mom settle into the house before heading to college at the University of Illinois, Champaign-

Urbana campus. The choice of Mom's and Dad's *alma mater* was easy, since Momma Nellie's house in Champaign remained our "permanent" address over the years, making me eligible to attend as an in-state student. Ron and Yvonne started school in the fall and with Mom and Dad established a household routine.

It was during this time Charles almost lost his perfect record. An officer and a gentleman, he prided himself in being well spoken and never used profanity. Sitting around the dinner table one evening, he became fed up listening to Ron and Yvonne bellyaching about something trivial. He glared from one to the other in foreboding silence, and then he blew.

"Well, tough...ah...huh...(the family waited in horror as he struggled)...ahhhhh...umm...(he finally blurted)...TITTY!!!!"

He looked at his shocked family who stole glances at one another, but dared not speak. At the relief of knowing his record was tarnished, but in tact, it was clear Frances was tickled and wrestling to suppress laughter. Somehow Ron and Yvonne managed to choke down the rest of their dinner having totally forgotten what they were fussing about. It was a close call. Ron and Yvonne had never seen Dad so exasperated or speechless, and though I missed the moment, I can appreciate it.

In Kansas City at Central Air Defense Force Headquarters, Charles filled a position in the Directorate of Logistics, with responsibility for assigned aircraft and missiles. Central territory ranged from the Arizona gulf region across the country's midland to Florida. Charles, and the officers and airmen reporting to him, monitored compliance with regulations, went into the field to examine how craft were maintained, and inspected the quality of work performed. Sometimes, testing called for planes to be deployed to simulate enemy penetration. The exercises gave Charles the welcome opportunity to fly. During drills, pilots of defending aircraft scrambled to intercept and identify, then returned to base to land for recovery operations and second wave responses.

The first year of college I spent Christmas break in Kansas City. After the holiday, Dad and I braved a snowstorm to get me back to school on roads that were icy and hazardous. Rather than taking the wheel, Dad wanted me to gain experience driving in these difficult conditions and coached me through tense miles of slow progress. Coming around a slow-moving vehicle on a single lane road, the car lost traction, entered a skid and rolled into a ditch. I blacked out for a time.

Coming to, I realized Dad was okay and except for a missing earring and shoe, I also appeared to be in one piece. Passersby helped us right the small car and return it to the highway. At a nearby gas station, Dad determined the car needed minor repairs which could not be accomplished before the next morning. Another car in the station displayed a U. of I. window sticker and to my shock and amazement Dad secured a ride from total strangers, white graduate students who took me on to Champaign and put me up in their dorm for the night.

Still in a daze when Dad arrived the next day, I did not object when he suggested Mom didn't need to know the details of the harrowing event. The following year I was happy to travel by train during the holidays.

In April '65, everyday activities were punctuated by a special occasion. Dad accompanied me down the aisle and gave my hand in marriage to William Yancy Smith. The romance which budded three years before had blossomed into full grown love and a commitment to be together as Bill graduated from the University of Illinois and was commissioned as a lieutenant in the U. S. Army. We married shortly after. A relative told me she had expected to get the announcement of my college graduation before the announcement of my wedding. If Dad felt that way, he did not say so. In the pictures of the wedding party, he and I are smiling. Behind those smiles are the unspoken thoughts of a father letting go and the joy of a daughter so absorbed in her new life, she does not know her father's feelings.

In Kansas City, life continued with the usual cadence of school, work, church, social and civic activities. Across the globe in Southeast Asia, things were far from usual. There hadn't been peace since conflicts between the Vietcong and the democratic government of South Vietnam erupted into fighting in 1957 after France's withdrawal. The United States supported the South Vietnamese government with money, weapons and military advisors, but in 1964 President Lyndon Johnson accused North Vietnam of sending military troops to aid the Vietcong and pledged U.S. troops to help fight the communists.

In 1967, Charles was nominated for assignment as Chief, Joint Plans and Operations, USAF Latin American Mission, requiring language school and service stationed in Nicaragua. For such higher level assignments, a request for nominations went out to commands. Once nominated, an alert from administration or personnel was sent indicating the pending transfer. For some reason, the first order was changed and Charles' name was submitted for assignment in Operations Branch at the Pentagon, but before he could report a third set of orders was issued and he was instead one of those to go to Southeast Asia.

His son-in-law, now on active duty, drew the only hardship assignment that could keep him out of Vietnam. He was on a tour of duty in Korea. Midway through his year at Camp Casey not far from Souel, Bill made plans for a stateside leave and Charles arranged to meet him on the west coast and fly him home. On June 30, Charles flew a T-39 to Alameda Naval Station and picked up his passenger.

I was waiting on the tarmac when they landed at Richards-Gebaur. The only thing that increased my excitement at seeing Bill after a six month separation was the pride I felt watching the two men most central in my life emerge from the plane and walk toward me side by side. My father delivered my husband to me and I felt like the most fortunate woman on earth.

Preparation for war in Vietnam would be arduous. Once Charles was reassigned, the family could no longer live on base, so he and Frances purchased a home in Sheritan Estates, a subdivision in southeast Kansas City, and moved in December 1966. The following month Charles reported to Shaw Air Force Base in South Carolina for reconnaissance ground school in class 67-4R.

Reconnaissance was new to Charles. There were two squadrons of sixteen crews who prepared to fly the RF-4C in Vietnam, the 16th Tactical Reconnaissance Squadron (TRS) which Charles would command and the 12th TRS to be based in Thailand. The "Phantom," as the RF-4C was known, had been stripped of its customary armament and refitted with surveillance equipment. Its primary job was to take aerial photos. Without guns, speed was its defense. This fighter jet had two seats, the pilot sat in front and an equipment/radar operator occupied the rear. Relying on the equipment operator, an integral part of the mission, was also new to Charles, who had single-handedly performed all mission requirements before. Without questioning whether or not he liked the change, Charles focused on the training that would allow him to accomplish the mission in a two crew relationship.

After Shaw AFB, Charles transferred to Mountain Home Air Force Base, Idaho, for aircraft checkout. The crew studied aircraft systems. Airborne they practiced maneuvers and learned the nuances of high and low altitude reconnaissance. At night, infrared equipment was used to sense and record thermal patterns or at times flares were fired to illuminate a target for photographing. Timing was critical to get to target, get the pictures, and get them back to base.

Training complete, Charles transferred to Fairchild Air Force Base outside Spokane, Washington for winter survival training. There was snow, snow and more snow in the wilderness where he was released to survive on knowledge and wits. The few rations in his pack had to be supplemented with berries, fish or other sustenance found in nature. At night he built a campfire for warmth and with hope of drying out his socks before the next day's trek. He melted snow for water. Exposure to smoke and flame caused an eye injury, but the endurance test continued. Reaching the designated rendezvous point, more hurdles awaited to test his stamina and physical limits. He faced confinement, grilling and interrogation a prisoner of war (POW) would undergo in enemy hands. Basic survival training completed, a week of jungle survival lay ahead.

The war in Southeast Asia was different than Europe or Korea. American soldiers were in unfamiliar territory in swamps and dense jungles. It was hard for them to know which villagers were friend and which were foe, making them vulnerable and paranoid at the same time. Extraordinary preparation was needed in response to these special challenges.

Frances expressed her dismay that Charles would be called upon to defend his country in a third war. She fumed.

"How much blood do they (the military) want!"

Charles did not question the call.

"I never volunteered, but when it comes you take it."

Military service was his life's work and he remained steadfast and loyal to his country. Charles knew patriotism often called for sacrifice. Again, he demonstrated courage and allegiance. Characteristically, he chose to look at a bright side. He was happy to be flying.

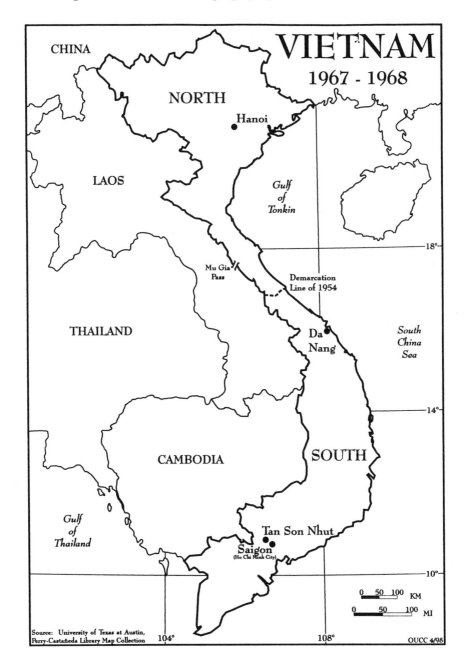

CHINA

VIETNAM
1967 - 1968

NORTH

Hanoi

LAOS

Gulf
of
Tonkin

—18°—

Mu Gia
Pass

Demarcation
Line of 1954

THAILAND

Da
Nang

South
China
Sea

—14°—

CAMBODIA

SOUTH

Gulf
of
Thailand

Tan Son Nhut

Saigon
(Ho Chi Minh City)

—10°—

0   50   100   KM
0   50   100   MI

Source: University of Texas at Austin,
Perry-Castañeda Library Map Collection   104°

108°

OUCC 4/98

XIV: The War in Vietnam

1967-1968

● In January 1968, North Vietnamese communists launched the Tet Offensive attacking numerous targets throughout South Vietnam.

● On April 4, 1968, Dr. Martin Luther King, Jr. was assassinated in Memphis, Tennessee, unleashing violent reaction in cities across the nation.

I n late May, 1967 Charles was on his way to the combat zone. His first stop "in theater" was the Philippines. There jungle survival trials recreated circumstances he would face if trapped behind enemy lines or shot down in hostile territory in Vietnam. He slept camouflaged in the jungle's underbrush and concealed himself during daylight as he cautiously made his way to the arranged rendezvous point.

Charles reported for his third combat duty on May 25, 1967 as Commander of the 16th Tactical Reconnaissance Squadron (TRS) at Tan Son Nhut Air Base, Republic of South Vietnam (RSVN). It was monsoon season. Everything stayed drenched, but soon Charles learned to ignore wet clothes and shoes. When the sun appeared, its intensity was quick drying. Metal insignia was not worn on uniforms and everything was finished in black to avoid easy detection, if downed in enemy territory.

Facilities consisted of wing headquarters, communications, a personal equipment room for flight gear, the flight planning room, intelligence section, weather office and the flight line with the RF-4s. Reconnaissance missions were flown round the clock with tactical intelligence gathered night and day to feed the constant need for information. Aerial photos were instrumental in pinpointing enemy infiltration and targets for offensive strikes. Counting flight planning, flying time, and debriefing after the flights, the squadron was on duty for a 16 to 17 hour period each day. Flying and sleeping quickly became main activities, with crews sometimes completing two missions per day.

Charles did a great deal of flying and usually with the same weapons system operator, Lt. Lynn Jorgensen. Their missions were primarily over the northern part of South Vietnam, although some were over Laos and North Vietnam. The most dangerous assignments were in Mu Gia Pass. The pass through mountainous country was considered a major infiltration route and therefore a frequent reconnaissance target. Difficult at best, the missions in Mu Gia Pass were especially hazardous when it was raining or foggy because then Charles and Jorgensen relied strictly on radar to locate targets, set course and guide them through the mountains.

"It made me a believer in the guy in the back seat."

When the Vietcong or North Vietnamese threw ground fire, speed was the Phantom's only protection. During night flights, the crew could see tracers coming up behind them. They would get to targets at high altitude, then drop down and fly at 360 knots at low altitude in patterns to photograph the area, increasing the speed to 420 or 460 knots over highly defended territory. Depending on the target and conditions, no two "recce" (reconnaissance) missions were alike and each had its unique dangers.

As squadron commander, Charles was responsible for all activities and when not flying or physically present at the facilities, he was on call. The squadron officers were billeted in a U.S. leased villa called Sam's in Saigon, about three or four miles from base. Charles rode a motorcycle for the first time because it provided the easiest means for getting back and forth.

Late in 1967, the 16th Squadron performed a special mission over Laos which Charles and his systems operator took. It was a day reconnaissance assignment over a road suspected as an enemy infiltration route. He received no intelligence of heavy defenses. Coming in for low altitude surveillance over the target, their plane was hit by ground fire from a large-millimeter gun. With fluid streaming from the left wing, Charles knew the situation was serious. Adrenaline was pumping as he put on more speed to get out of the line of fire. All of his training was called into play and while he was performing, he was too busy to dwell on the danger. The good Lord willing, they would get home in one piece.

He made the decision to abort the mission and divert to Da Nang, a base on the sea coast far north of Tan Son Nhut. The way to safety was over enemy territory and the chance of survival was greatly diminished if they had to eject. All senses were alert and every minute he stayed aloft drew him nearer to safety. With the base finally in sight and not knowing the extent of damage to hydraulics or landing gear, Charles prepared for a risky landing.

F-4s were equipped with a drag chute which was deployed upon landing. Without it, even a 9000 foot runway was not adequate distance to stop the craft safely. Deploying the drag chute would be of no help to Charles if there were problems with the plane's brakes. In contact with the tower controller, Charles requested an approach end tail hook landing.

Emergency vehicles were poised. He dropped the hook on approach and continued his dissent...300 feet...200 feet.... At 175 miles per hour he dropped hard onto the runway. An eternity passed before he felt the rough tug of a secure catch. The plan worked. Safely on the ground, Charles, with his systems operator, unloaded the film before the aircraft was towed to the maintenance area.

They hopped a ride with an army general on the way to Saigon in a T-39, a twin engine executive jet, and returned to Tan Son Nhut later the same day. When he got back, Charles turned in his film and was flying another mission the next day.

U.S. strength in South Vietnam approached a half a million personnel in 1967. By the end of the year, 75 MiGs had been downed in air-to air combat in the North at a cost of 25 U.S. aircraft. With U.S. and Allied forces battling the Vietcong and North Vietnamese, the enemy had not won a major victory. North Vietnam decided on another strategy.

The Vietcong used the New Year holiday to launch a surprise attack known as the Tet Offensive on January 31, 1968. They attacked throughout the country, striking numerous installations, cities and airfields simultaneously. When fighting broke out in the area where U.S. troops were housed in Saigon, the villa was attacked at the outset and only six pilots were on base, Charles among them. He and Lt. Col. Ray Renfro were at squadron headquarters for early flights and on base with four others. The rest pinned down at the villa had to stay, cut off without food or means of protection until rescued by an army personnel carrier.

The crews on base flew all squadron missions for three days, before conditions allowed relief. Hutches were quickly built for them to live in. When the Vietcong started mortaring the base, there were foxholes for some protection, but no way to predict where the shells would land. With a chance to rest, Charles stayed in bed with a helmet over his head.

Six or seven of the 16th's planes were hit on the ground in revetments constructed to protect them. Some burned and others sustained shrapnel damage.

In this fateful circumstance, the 16th did not lose a mission. Unbeknownst to him, these conditions helped propel Charles into the record books. As the stranded fliers reported, they relieved him and the beleaguered crews, but not before he had flown many back to back missions.

As battle ensued, telephone lines were cut and there was no radio communication. Mortars, rifle fire, grenades and rockets were directed at the living quarters as well as the base. There was fighting in the streets and though the roof of the villa seemed deceptively safe, it was there Charles lost one of his navigators that first night. A bullet from an unknown assailant struck him in the back.

"Loss had to be dealt with, an onerous task of war."

Initially, the enemy made gains, but the offensive failed in late February, after having a significant impact on people back home watching the nightly news. The U.S. sent more troops to South Vietnam in an attempt to accelerate an end to the conflict and the withdrawal of its forces. To induce North Vietnam leaders to return to the Paris peace table, President Johnson limited bombings north of the 20th parallel.

For political reasons, the use of air power was constrained in Vietnam. The Air Force mounted a protracted counter-insurgence effort against a determined and elusive enemy. Tactical aircraft such as the F-4 Phantom II performed a variety of roles from aerial combat to close air support. The F-105 Thunderchief specialized in bombing raids against North Vietnam, while B-52s carpet bombed remote jungle strongholds. Tactical intelligence was constantly needed to identify the targets. The B-52s flew sorties to Laos where targets were trucks sometimes hunted down and destroyed one by one.

The Air Force did not experience fighting in Vietnam the same as ground soldiers. Despite the need to contend with jungle heat and local skirmishes, pilots for the most part took off and returned to base, conducting their combat missions in the skies overhead. Their objectives were comparatively clear and well defined.

Ground troops fought a very different war. As Vietcong advanced into an area, some villagers were sympathetic to their cause and others were not, but both stayed behind reluctant to leave their homes in a time of great upheaval. Likewise, as forces of the South Vietnamese government gained territory, it was easy for the Vietcong to disguise themselves in newly captured villages. Too often, there was no way to tell friend from foe until it was too late. The swamps and jungles were formidable enemies which sapped the energy and spirit of fighters who were unaccustomed to this confounding warfare. Charles had great empathy for soldiers contending with such daunting obstacles. His task was to secure the best possible information, and he did so with the hope it would ease their plight.

The first day Lt. Col. Renfro met Charles, he began to judge the character of his commander.

"I called the 16th TRS and advised them where I was. In a few minutes, Lt. Col. McGee arrived in a pick-up and takes me to the squadron operations building. Now he could have sent one of the Lts. (lieutenants), but he came himself and made me feel welcome....He personally introduced me to each officer and airman in the operations office...."

There were other occasions when Charles pitched in, like the clean up at Sam's when crews moved on base after being stranded during the Tet offensive.

"Most commanders would have had a detail of airmen do this dirty, messy work, but not him. The mission performance was foremost in his thinking and he was not too proud to apply himself to such a humble task."

This is how Charles approached the job and in the eyes of his supervisor of flying (SOF), Lt. Col. Renfro, he got results.

"Never did ...(the flight scheduling officer)... have any trouble getting crews to fly some of our most hazardous missions. I attribute this attitude to the example and leadership of our C.O. (Charles McGee). He also had the utmost respect and cooperation of the flight line maintenance people. As a result, we had outstanding maintenance on our airplanes."

In May 1968, Charles flew his 173rd and final mission in Vietnam. On landing, he was greeted with the customary fire truck shower and bottle of champagne, most of which went on and not in one very happy flier. Other pilots celebrated with him. Each ritual honoring their predecessors took them one step closer to their own departure, with the ever-present unspoken caveat, God willing.

Charles and the men who served with him were not focused on the growing unrest about the war among Americans at home. Their attention had to be on the job at hand. Their lives and the lives of other servicemen depended on it. Lacking a declaration of war, and hampered by political restrictions, Vietnam would be an example that military power under political auspices seldom, if ever, finds a winning solution. History would later record that more than two and one half million Americans served and over 58,000 died in a war many never understood.

XV: Supersonic Speed

1968-1972

● Richard M. Nixon became President in January, 1969, and soon accelerated the withdrawal of U.S. troops from Vietnam.

● In the 1970s the Air Force modernized aircraft and missiles and expanded its role in space, making progress in satellite-based communications, reconnaissance, warning, weather and navigation systems.

For his service in the war in Vietnam, Charles received the Legion of Merit, Distinguished Flying Cross, and several Air Medals. By the time the review of his record was completed and these medals awarded, he was back in Germany with Frances and Yvonne. Frances had not been at all interested in returning to Europe. The thought of leaving home and friends once more was depressing, but at Charles' urging she pulled herself together and played the part of the dutiful officer's wife.

Ron was in Topeka attending college at Kansas University (KU) against the advice of high school counselors who patronizingly told him to attend a trade school for a few years. Determined to study aeronautics, he didn't listen and not only gained entrance to KU, but was also admitted into the competitive engineering program. Lewis Sr. and Marcella moved to Kansas City to "house sit" while Charles and Frances were in Europe.

Dad was different after Vietnam. When he left he was hearty and fair-skinned with dark trimmed hair. The man who came home was lean and crispy brown with silvery hair, someone I had never seen before. His eyes were not as bright and even though he sounded the same, I had the feeling he was working hard to hold a regular conversation.

It was difficult for me to imagine how Dad could have changed so much in one year and I was worried for him, however the most troubling changes were short lived. William and I were living in married student housing at the University of Illinois and our daughter Tesha, Dad's first grandchild, was almost two years old. I'm sure Dad felt I too had changed. In ensuing years I understood better the nature of change, but that has not dulled the startling impression Dad made when he returned from Vietnam.

Charles initial assignment was in Hiedelberg, Germany with the United States Army Europe (USAEUR) and 7th Army as Air Liaison Officer. At Hiedelberg in the fall of 1968, he observed two anniversaries. One was 26 years of marriage (he spent his silver wedding anniversary in Southeast Asia) and the second was his silver anniversary marking 25 years of military service.

Early the following year, he celebrated his promotion to full colonel. As the time of the promotion approached, Frances was giddy with excitement. The new rank could not officially be pinned on before the effective date, so Charles and Frances, not wanting to break the rules, set the alarm clock for midnight and woke Yvonne up for an official family pinning ceremony. Pictures were taken to record the momentous event and, until now, only the three of them knew that below his uniform jacket, Dad was wearing pajama bottoms.

The "bird colonel" rank led to his assignment as Chief of Maintenance for the 50th Tactical Fighter Wing at Hahn Air Base, Germany. Hahn was a small air base tucked in beautiful mountains near the Luxembourg border. In some ways the assignment was an exhilarating chapter in Charles' flying experience. In others it signaled the beginning of the end of a distinguished military career.

Excitement came with the introduction of the newly assigned F-4E. This craft was planned for air defense work, as compared to the Wing's F-4C ("Wild Weasel"), used for electronic surveillance, and the F-4D model, fulfilling the normal tactical fighter role. The E model had the latest electronic features and a more powerful engine. The advent of these state of the art aircraft heightened Charles' enthusiasm for flying.

"You knew right away you were in the Cadillac, not the Model-T."

The F-4 was capable of achieving a speed of mach 2 (twice the speed of sound). In breaking the sound barrier for the first time, Charles experienced velocity at its most thrilling. He felt himself pinned to the seat and the stiffness of the controls caused by the dynamic pressure. Without an outside point of reference, there was no way to grasp the marvel of it. A glance at his fuel gauge though provided a true measure. Above mach 1, he was burning fuel far faster than the normal rate and could literally see the indicator needle dropping. Fully fueled, at maximum power the flying time in the F-4 was about 32 minutes, while during normal cruise it was over two hours.

At supersonic speeds, added velocity became harder to achieve.

"You reach mach 1 rather quickly. From that point to 1.5 takes longer and then even longer to see 1.7........ 1.8.......... and the goal, mach 2 on the air speed indicator."

Charles explained the accumulating mass of compacted air in front of the plane creates greater and greater resistance and the controls become stiff, as if frozen.

While Dad was breaking the sound barrier, Ron was studying about it. He joined the Air Force ROTC program at KU. With Vietnam protesters and dissension boiling, joining didn't serve to make him very popular. Nevertheless, he moved one step closer to his objective of one day flying.

Many years later, Dad and Ron attempted to explain to me what it was like to be at the controls of a plane flying faster than the speed of sound. We talked about the sonic boom created when the pressure wave of compressed air reaches ground issuing a loud report and the way they were propelled forward in their seat when the afterburners shut down. From the look on their faces and light shining in their eyes as they conversed, I could tell any attempt to truly understand would fall short.

At Hahn, Charles and the other senior officers were called to a personnel briefing. On the surface it seemed routine. The Air Force had completed a study and was using briefings to disseminate findings and new directives. The problem was the relatively short time in grade for the general officers. Based on existing policies for retirement, if the rank of general was not an attainment by 30 years, retirement was mandatory. Even with the rank of general, retirement was mandatory at 35 years. As a result, generals tended to serve only three to five years. The study concluded the investment was greater than the return. The solution adopted was to pass over a two year group of officers approaching the promotion zone and reach down to advance a younger group to be considered for general officer ranks.

It happened that Tuskegee Airmen along with white officers in line for a star were in the group affected by this decision. The truth was there were fewer Lieutenant Colonels and Colonels among the Tuskegee Airmen which was indicative of earlier advancement policies for black officers. To this point, Charles had made satisfactory career progress, but this was not the case across the board.

The military had the power to adjust its work force. Those Airmen negatively affected by the policy change did not know if they were inadvertent or intended victims. No evidence has been brought to light to confirm or dispel speculation, but the coincidence leaves a significant unanswered question in the final military chapter of these trailblazing patriots.

There were new challenges faced by Charles and Frances in Hahn. Until diagnosed and treated, Frances suffered with serious fatigue brought on by potassium depletion. Yvonne, 16 years old, was struggling to establish her identity and independence. She was a light-skinned black teenager, living the privileged life of an officer's kid, in a white power structure. At the same time she knew a black power revolution was in full swing back home. None of the standard answers worked for her and she didn't follow the rules, landing her in trouble on more than one occasion.

Decades later Yvonne still harbored guilt that somehow her troubles were the black mark on Dad's record which kept him from getting his star. There were competing explanations.

Yvonne, like me, was sent to boarding school in Wiesbaden because Hahn did not have an accredited program for juniors and seniors. Frances was troubled by the separation from her youngest child, particularly during the difficult and quickly changing times.

In 1970, Charles traveled with the family to the States for the wedding of his son, Ron, to Patricia Scott in Topeka. In the fall of that year, Charles was completing his third year of duty in Germany and due to rotate Stateside. His assignment was to Air Force Communications Service (AFCS) which was moved from Scott Air Force Base near St. Louis, Missouri, to Richards-Gebaur AFB. With that stroke of good fortune, he and Frances would move back to their Kansas City home. Lewis Sr. and Marcella found a place in a retirement village in Merritt Island, Florida. After Yvonne's graduation in 1971, Charles took his family home.

Returning to R-G, Charles took the post of Director of Maintenance Engineering for AFCS. With the position came responsibility for communication systems, including military satellites now circling the globe. After three years in Europe, there was a lot of personal catching up to do with family and friends. Tesha was almost five and there was a second granddaughter, Damona Gay, named after her paternal great grandmother. She was almost two years old when they saw her for the first time at Ron's wedding.

Passing through Illinois Charles and Frances stopped in Batavia to visit his sister Ruth, her husband Jacob "Jake" Downs and their five sons. I had visited with the Downs family several times while Mom and Dad were overseas. It was a way to keep in touch with relatives with my parents and siblings so far away. Ruth never ceased to amaze me with the energy she poured into her work and boys. Once they visited my tiny apartment in Champaign, bringing food in bowls too big to wash in my kitchen sink. I never forgot the Thanksgiving evening in Batavia when she put 42 pork chops on a rotisserie grill just after dark, in case somebody wanted "a snack" before bed. Her growing boys loved to eat.

That visit in 1971 was the last time Charles would see his sister alive. She died unexpectedly the following Spring, not having reached her fiftieth birthday. At her funeral, her boys sat shoulder to shoulder and took up an entire church pew. She had given them a solid start and they would have to move on without her. So would Charles, now the sole surviving child of Lewis Sr. and Ruth McGee.

Good things were recorded in 1971 though. Yvonne started college at Hampton Institute as a mass media arts major. On October 14, 1971, Charles' first grandson, Damon Yancy Smith, was born into the family. A proud Grandma ("Ga") and Grandpa ("Pa Pa Gee") visited us several weeks later. Ronald defied predictions and graduated from KU with a degree in aerospace engineering. He started active duty in the Air Force in December of that year. In addition to Dad's determination and perseverance, he had inherited a desire to fly and gained admittance to pilot training at Lorado Air Force Base in Texas. When he finished the program, Dad flew to Lorado to pin on Ron's wings. During the pinning the first pair of wings was broken, by tradition representing each pilots first accident now banished in the ceremonial act.

The ceremony offered a time to reflect on his own career. Charles' wings had been pinned on by Frances almost three decades earlier. Since then he had added a star above the wings when he made senior pilot, and finally a wreath surrounding the star when he became a command pilot. His chest was covered with rows of medals commemorating distinguished service in three wars and thirty years. There had been tremendous stereotypes to overcome. Charles and his fellow black Airmen confronted them and because they were resolute, he could now see his son, standing on the shoulders of his forebearers, reach for a higher rung.

Charles' military career was approaching an end. He and other Tuskegee Airmen watched younger men with less time in grade move to the ranks of general officer, while they began to contemplate civilian life. For Charles, there may have been disappointment, but no bitterness or regrets. His military career was one of accomplishment and distinction. He had served well. For Frances the idea was a welcome one. For so long she had been bound by the dictates of service life. The idea of retirement meant no more separation and greater freedom. She looked forward to fewer demands.

During Dad's last year in the Air Force, Major General Paul Stony, head of Communication Service, asked Charles to take command of Richards-Gebaur AFB. Col. Aubrey Gaskins was too ill to lead and Stony selected Charles to be his replacement.

"I always wanted this task, so on June 24, 1972, I got my opportunity and with it a key to the city of Belton, the same place that denied me housing less than two decades before."

Charles agreed, and assumed command. He became the first black to hold a stateside Air Force Wing and Base command.

Another black officer, Colonel William Earl Brown Jr., was appointed to a similar position in Arizona shortly thereafter. Charles was still breaking barriers and setting precedents when his active duty military career ended on January 31, 1973.

XVI: Tuskegee Airmen, Inc.

1973-1979

- Gerald R. Ford succeeded Richard Nixon as President of the United States after Nixon resigned in the wake of the Watergate scandal.
- General Daniel "Chappie" James, Jr., the first U.S. Air Force African-American 4-star general, became Commander in Chief, North American Air Defense Command and Aerospace Defense Command in September, 1975.
- Jimmy Carter defeated Gerald Ford in his bid for election and assumed the Presidency in 1977.
- The U.S. Supreme Court outlawed racial quotas in a suit brought by Allan Bakke, a white man denied admission to medical school at University of California, Davis.

History had been silent on the exploits of the Tuskegee Airmen. They themselves were anything but quiet. Regional gatherings began to occur in New York, Washington D.C., Detroit and Los Angeles reuniting Airmen from the original group of pilots and their support crew. Some of these men and women, like Charles, had remained in the military service during the post World War II era and spearheaded the desegregation of the armed forces of the United States. Three of these pioneers were ultimately elevated to flag rank: Lt. General B.O. Davis Jr., Major General Lucius Theus and General Daniel "Chappie" James, this nation's first black four-star general. Many had returned to civilian life and earned positions of leadership and respect as businessmen, corporate executives, religious and political leaders, lawyers, doctors, bankers, and educators.

There were others interested in the past and future of blacks in aviation who joined the initial trailbrazers. Charles attended each of their gatherings and worked with a nucleus of leaders who founded a national organization to preserve the heritage of the Tuskegee Airmen and provide a pathway for future generations of black aviators. With great satisfaction he witnessed the birth of the association in 1972 and chaired the constitution and by-laws committee charged with drawing up the founding documents. Groundwork was laid to end nearly thirty years of anonymity.

The association incorporated becoming Tuskegee Airmen, Inc. (TAI) in 1974.

Organized as a nonpolitical, non-military, not-for-profit national entity, TAI exists to motivate and inspire young Americans to be active participants in society and its democratic processes and aspire to aviation and aerospace careers.

Retirement from military service opened new doors for Charles. Within a month of separation, he accepted an appointment as Director of Real Estate and Purchasing for ISC Industries. Later, he also became Vice President for Real Estate for Interstate Securities Company, a subsidiary of ISC Financial Corporation. It seemed a far cry from work he did in the Air Force, but in reality his administrative training and experience in the military made him well suited. In one situation he managed aircraft, missiles and satellites; in the other it was buildings and properties. To come up to speed in the technical aspects of his new job, Charles enrolled in business law courses and studied real estate, earning a broker's license.

Headquartered in Kansas City, ISC was a corporation with holdings throughout the country. The company leased aircraft to ferry executives from place to place, a bonus for Charles because he served as second pilot as requested by the company president whenever he was aboard. Most trips were from headquarters in Kansas City to places were ISC held subsidiary interests. Some were same day excursions to nearby locations in Kansas and others were as far away as Florida and Washington State, where Charles took care of leasing and furnishing matters for newly acquired holdings. During the ISC years he added the Beach King Air, a turbo prop, to his flying portfolio and made a landing in a Lear Jet.

Contrary to Frances' expectations, life after the military was just as demanding of Charles' time. He was as busy as ever. That blow was softened, however, by perks ISC offered. Her eyes danced when she relayed news of the first impressive annual bonus.

"I'm talking serious money, not a little token. It's in the six figure range! Not five. Six!"

Away from the office, days were full with new ventures, founding of the Heart of America Chapter of TAI among them. Through TAI, fraternal organizations and the church, Charles lived his convictions. Exhibiting confidence, commitment and dignity, he influenced others to join in efforts to improve the lives of people they touched.

Charles also kept up with military news, noting with great satisfaction "Chappie" James' promotion to 4-star general in September of 1975 and his subsequent assignment as Commander in Chief, North American Air Defense Command and Aerospace Defense Command. Like Charles, he fought for his country in three wars and believed in America, mindful for both its strengths and weaknesses.

The five and a half years with ISC passed comfortably, but in the summer of 1978 all was not well with the company. People in the insurance division made some decisions which landed ISC in financial and legal difficulties. Charles was pretty close-mouthed about the matter but there was no mistaking his disappointment with the turn of events. It was very difficult for a man of principle to find himself in the midst of a controversy which carried legal implications for the company's executives. Charles was not implicated in any of the questionable dealings, which came as no surprise to anyone who knew him. Nevertheless he felt the stigma of being associated with a failed venture under possibly shady circumstances. He wasn't talking about it, but Frances acknowledged that some people involved would be indicted and, if convicted, could go to jail.

In the aftermath, ISC reorganized and sold Interstate Securities Company in the summer of 1978. Charles and other personnel were not continued, but a veteran of conflict, his past allowed him to withstand this disturbing chain of events. More than a survivor, he had become adept at turning adversity to advantage. The guiding principle was simple.

"Accentuate the positive; eliminate the negative."

The separation from ISC became an opportunity for Charles to focus on a lifelong ambition. Always a staunch believer in the value of education, he pursued formal training throughout the years. One thing he had wanted since his days at the University of Illinois eluded him, a college degree. His time at U. of I., Command and Staff School, studies while in Minnesota and recent courses while at ISC were credits toward a college diploma. A degree granting program was needed to pull them together. Columbia College in Columbia, Missouri, provided an extension program to meet the need. Returning to school was a labor of love for Charles. It didn't matter he was generation or more older than his classmates. He had the zeal and commitment of a man on a quest.

Charles earned a baccalaureate degree in June of 1979 with Dean's List honors. It was an achievement that rivaled others in a life of accomplishments, and with it came a strong sense of personal satisfaction. His commitment to education was enacted on another front as well. In 1979 TAI established its National Scholarship Fund. With his strong support over ensuing years, this permanent endowment, valued at more than a million dollars, would award hundreds of scholarships to students pursuing their dreams in the field of aviation.

"It's all about training and opportunity….an ongoing fight to find and develop the potential in all Americans."

After earning his degree, Charles accepted an administrative position with the City of Prairie Village, Kansas. That appointment was brief. After six months, he left to go to his father's bedside and be with him in the last weeks of his life. Living in Pullman, Washington, with his wife and step daughter, Joan Harris, Lewis Sr. had become terminally ill with prostate cancer and within weeks following surgery died of the disease. His body was cremated and his ashes interred in Arlington National Cemetery. Shortly after his death, Charles returned to Kansas City to begin a new chapter in his own life.

XVII: Contributions and Tributes

1980-1994

- The Regan-Bush years, ushered in with the 1980 election of Ronald W. Reagan, ended with the 1992 presidential election when Bill Clinton defeated George Bush in his bid for a second term.
- The Berlin Wall dividing East and West Germany was torn down, reuniting the country in 1989.
- After 27 years of imprisonment in South Africa, Nelson Mandela gained his freedom on February 11, 1990.
- Air power, delivering an arsenal of precision guided munitions, played a decisive role in the 1991 Operation Desert Storm victory over Iraq's Saddam Hussein.
- After a decade of civil rights gains and losses, the first racially based riots in years erupted in Los Angeles and other cities following the acquittal of white police officers in the videotaped beating of Rodney King, a African-American.

Over the years Charles had volunteered his services to Kansas City in a number of capacities, including the Armory Advisory Board and the Richards-Gebaur AFB Reuse Committee. As a cost cutting measure, Richards-Gebaur was stripped of active duty Air Force units. Activities were greatly reduced on the once thriving base and Frances, having fond memories of their time there, found it depressing to return for shopping at the base exchange and commissary or social events at the Officers' Club.

Charles' network of friends and acquaintances grew to include Tom Lowensen, Personnel Director for the city. Through this contact, Charles' name emerged when a manager was being sought for the Kansas City Downtown Airport.

While he looked considerably younger, he was sixty years old when he started the job in 1980. It was a great move for him; "super" as he recalled. It gave him the chance to combine his management skill and love for aviation.

Due to location and convenience, the Downtown Airport was heavily trafficked with more take offs and landings than many large commercial operations. In addition to a small commercial feeder line, the airport supported corporate and training aircraft and leased space to numerous tenants including an aviation school and the Federal Aviation Authority (FAA) for administration of the control tower. Charles' small, well-knit crew managed responsibilities ranging from runway lighting to airport security. Everything down to snow removal was highly organized, so much so that the airport never had to be closed while under his direction.

I visited the airport during a stay in Kansas City. Dad invited Bill and me to join him for lunch. We toured the facility beforehand and as we sat in the restaurant overlooking the tarmac, I had a glimpse of my Dad in his natural surroundings. He was comfortably in command and it was clear people enjoyed working for him.

Charles was in his element and again having fun, but at the same time he could not be oblivious to Frances' growing frustration. This was his third position since retiring from the Air Force; they were still postponing the things Frances hoped they would do together. She had raised her family and cared for Momma Nellie, who lived with them in her final years. She was an avid seamstress and very active in the church, but there was more she wanted to do with Charles, things like additional travel and visiting the kids and their growing families. Ron and his wife, Pat, had a daughter, Erin. When Ron finished his six and a half year stint with the Air Force, unlike black pilots in Charles' generation, he was able to continue flying as a commercial pilot for Braniff Airlines. Ron and his family had moved from Texas to Denver and Yvonne lived in Baltimore where she was working as a television editor/producer. My family and I lived in Athens, Ohio, where Bill and I worked for Ohio University. With the children and grandchildren so spread out, it was hard to fit visits into long weekends and periodic vacations.

Like Momma Nellie, Mom loved to fish and this interest had also taken a back seat to Dad's career. So after two and a half years as Airport Manager, Dad "retired" for the last time. Even then, he did not stop contributing. His motto was and remained, "Do while you can." He continued to serve the city as a member, and several years chairman, of its Municipal Assistance Corporation and charter member of the Aviation Advisory Commission. With his background, the personally rewarding work greatly benefited the city.

Charles did however attend to some of Frances' interests. They enjoyed many long hours along the shore of nearby streams and lakes, even though Charles' preference may have been going to a golf course. That was one thing Frances did not care to do: "hit a golf ball, just to go find it to hit again."

In between their travels and days on the lake shore or river bank, Charles dedicated himself to furthering the cause of TAI. After two years as Vice President of the organization, he moved up to assume the presidency in 1984 and stayed in that position for a second term.

In 1985, Charles presided over dedication of a permanent memorial at the Air Force Museum, honoring Tuskegee Airman and their heroic achievements. Bill and I drove to Dayton to be on hand for the program which included a tour of the museum, a formal ceremony and aerial salute during a formation fly by. It was truly a moving program. I couldn't have been prouder or happier for Dad and the others so deservingly recognized.

Other tributes followed. In 1987, a permanent museum was dedicated at Historic Fort Wayne in Detroit, Michigan, in honor of the Tuskegee Airmen. The Smithsonian Institution commissioned a series of prints for its Black Wings exhibit. In 1988,

Mom and Dad attended the ceremony when an eight foot memorial statue was unveiled at the Air Force Academy in Colorado Springs, Colorado. Ron was flying during the dedication, but later visited the site and read the words inscribed there: "Through their life, we have life."

Charles' presence was in great demand whether at these official ceremonies or working behind the scenes to move the next TAI initiative forward. He traveled as much on business as for pleasure, and Frances joined him selectively, more often staying behind when she didn't think her presence was needed. Several trips they made together were to Athens, Ohio, one when my youngest daughter, Charon, was born in May of 1988 and another in June, 1990, when I received my doctoral degree.

Although there are other things in my life which have pleased Dad, earning a Ph.D. ranks near the top of the list. Part of my satisfaction in reaching the goal was knowing how much it meant to him to have a "doctor" in the McGee family. He had high expectations for me. With him to set the example and encourage me along the way, how could I aim for anything less!

Charles and Frances traveled to Scott Air Force Base in Illinois in July, 1990, where Dad pinned on major's leaves at the promotion ceremony of Richard Hall. The two men first met in 1976 when Charles and several other Tuskegee Airmen were special guests at the Air Force Academy Speakers' Forum. Richard, a young cadet in the audience, was from a small town in northern Louisiana and didn't know much about aviation or black pilots who flew in the second world war. Listening to them talk about their experience flying and integrating the armed services, a new world opened to Hall. Their presence was commanding and their story compelling. He met Charles and the others after the program.

"We were incredibly impressed and in awe (of their achievements)."

After graduation, Hall went on to pilot training, earning his wings in 1980. He didn't see Charles again until the TAI convention in New York City. Charles, then President of the association, was genuinely excited to know how Hall's career had progressed. Five years later, Charles was the one he wanted to pin on his major's leaves.

"Charles stood out as the ultimate role model. He gave me something to shoot for."

The following summer, Charles and Frances were in Atchison, Kansas, for Charles' induction into the Memory Lane Walkway of the International Forest of Friendship. Sponsored by the Harry S. Truman Chapter of the Air Force Association, his name was inscribed on the granite plaque embedded in the walkway along with 600 other aviation pioneers honored since the founding of the Forest of Friendship. Dad's inclusion and the day long celebration pleased them both immensely.

In October of 1992, Mom and Dad celebrated their 50th Wedding Anniversary at Lake of the Ozarks, Missouri. It was a perfect weekend; crisp fall weather and a gorgeous time of year, with foliage in full color. Mom dropped a fishing line in the lake just yards from the front door of the condominium and for that among other things she was truly appreciative.

Yvonne and I joined them and captured the occasion and its sublime surroundings on video tape. More memorable for me than the beauty of the time and place was the glow of their enduring love. I was profoundly grateful to be a part of it. Mom had considered and rejected other ways to celebrate their golden anniversary. One had been a trip to Austria and another a banquet with friends and family in Kansas City. On balance, she was very pleased with her choice and Dad was pleased to be doing what made her happy. It was a tranquil oasis in the midst of hectic lives which became even more poignant. Six months later Mom was diagnosed with the fatal illness which would claim her life.

The illness was aplastic anemia, a disease in which the body stops producing white blood cells. She and Dad had come to Ohio to help Bill and me through a health crisis of our own. Exhausted, Mom stopped in the emergency room before leaving the hospital where Bill had undergone surgery and, within the hour, she was herself hospitalized. I'll never forget Dad's return to Bill's room. When he saw doctors attending to Bill, he said he would wait in the corridor, asking me to step out when I could. His words were normal but something in his subdued manner alerted me. I went to find him as soon as I could. Shortly after, we were talking to Mom's doctors about blood transfusions and arrangements to transport her back to Kansas City.

With the benefit of frequent blood and platelet transfusions, Mom lived almost a year after her illness was diagnosed. Together they packed as much love into that year as they had in the ones before. Maybe even more. Even with the loss of a kidney and active diabetes, I'm not sure it occurred to any of us Dad would outlive Mom. Widows are more common than widowers. For the first time in their half century together, Dad needed to acquire a different set of survival skills to help Mom through her final months. As her health failed he cooked, cleaned and did the washing. He waited with her for hours on end at Research Hospital, where her blood count was tested weekly and transfusions were administered.

Over the course of the year, I saw hope fade from his eyes, but I never once heard him complain. When she was strong enough to travel, they visited family. When she wasn't, he washed her and fed her. When she could not be at home, he stayed by her bedside at the hospital.

Right up to the end, Mom did things to make life easier for all of us. In January 1994, she picked out her casket so that matter would be taken care of. Dad and I went with her and while we were there he took the liberty of giving me an idea of what he might want when the time came.

I marveled at my parents' infinite capacity to face life's greatest challenges with such practicality!

On February 22, 1994, Frances died. Her funeral was at Swope Parkway United Christian Church in Kansas City. At the internment service in the Chapel at Arlington National Cemetery, Charles sang Frances' favorite hymn, How Great Thou Art. There were some who thought he would not be able to do it. He did it perfectly.

There were those who worried for him as he pulled his life together after she was gone, and we hovered around him a bit closer than he might have liked.

If we had understood him better we would have known he had the strength to survive even this great loss.

His spirituality comforted him and his perseverance kept him on a course of purpose, which would continue to give meaning to his life. As father, church elder and Tuskegee Airman, slowly but surely, he re-engaged where he could make a contribution.

XVIII: One For The Record

1994-1997
- In 1994 Nelson Mandela was elected President of the Republic of South Africa.
- The post-Cold War Air Force participated in contingency operations, including humanitarian efforts in Somalia and Rwanda and peacekeeping assignments in the Balkans.
- The 1996 Summer Olympic Games held in Atlanta, Georgia, hosted more participating countries than ever before.
- A new rash of attacks on black churches in the South began in 1996.
- On September 18, 1997, the United States Air Force celebrated its 50th anniversary, commemorating a half century of achievements, honoring contributors and anticipating the challenges of global engagement in the 21st Century.

In August of 1994, Charles attended the TAI Convention in Atlanta, Georgia. As the banquet hall for the closing event filled with members of the Association and their families, including dozens of the original Airmen, the audience was not aware of the news they were about to receive. General Ronald Fogleman, Air Force Chief of Staff, was the keynote speaker for the event. He spoke receiving polite attention customary for such an occasion. Then he announced he brought special news to the gathering, news of an official pardon for men court-martialed in the aftermath of the Freeman Field demonstration fifty years earlier. *(In his book, The Freeman Field Mutiny, Lieutenant Colonel James Warren revealed a first hand account of the incident and the injustice of arrests of*

*black officers opposing segregationist policies at Freeman Field
in April 1945. His revelations were credited with playing a role
in securing the pardons.)*

A stir went through the crowd as the significance of Fogleman's words sank in. Spontaneous acclamation arose! The
impact was electrifying! A grave injustice was to be removed
from the record. Although it came late, and could not repair the
lives crippled by the impact of reprimands and dishonorable
discharges a half century before, it was a victory nonetheless.
Several of those in the audience had worked for years to
overturn these unfair convictions and were directly affected by
the pardon. All were deeply moved.

As if this news alone was not enough, still more was in store
that evening. Fogleman went on to praise the many great
contributions of the Tuskegee Airmen. Among them, he noted
there was an Airman in the audience who had the distinction of
having flown more fighter combat missions than any other pilot
in the three-war history of the Air Force. The buzz returned as
all present contemplated who that might be. Dad may have
been the most surprised when he heard his name.

"After fighting in World War II, Col. Chuck McGee went on
to fly and fight in Korea and in Vietnam. He racked up the
highest three-war total of fighter missions of any Air Force
aviator—409 missions.... An American hero and an Air Force
legend."

At 409 missions he held the record! Of course, he knew how
many missions he had flown, but did not know how that
number compared to other pilots. Though not many, there were
others who flew in the countries three most recent conflicts in
which there had been significant aerial combat. He surpassed
them all! Not a distinction one seeks; God willing, no other
flier will need to exceed it. It was one for the record!

Missouri Governor Mel Carnahan proclaimed April 4, 1995,
Tuskegee Airmen Day, in recognition of those "who overcame
insurmountable obstacles to demonstrate their courage and

patriotism." Charles was in Kansas City to witness this honor. Shortly after, surrounded in Kansas City by a host of friends but no family, he made the decision to leave his long-time home and move to Bethesda, Maryland, where he and Yvonne bought a house. Adding to her accomplishments as an Emmy Award winning television editor, Yvonne instructed scuba diving and was taking lessons to earn her pilot's license. Their busy schedules kept them away frequently, however, in times together they went to plays and concerts, visited friends, worked on TAI business and sustained family ties.

Tributes to the Tuskegee Airmen continued to give them their rightful place in history. On Veteran's Day in 1995, a tree was planted and plaque erected in the Arlington Cemetary Memorial Gardens. Yvonne was on hand to witness the solemn and majestic ceremony. On hallowed ground within this most serene national historic setting, the words are inscribed, "They accepted the challenge. A grateful nation will not forget."

Words spoken by the dignitaries gathered that day, including Lieutenant General B. O. Davis Jr., acknowledged that Tuskegee Airmen engaged and defeated two enemies, one abroad and one at home. In war, their record stands unsurpassed. In peace, they confronted prejudice, intolerance and injustice. In both cases they kept up the good fight, so America could emerge stronger and stand victorious. Victory achieved on the battlefield, they continue to make contributions in the struggle for civil rights and equality for all. Their recognition was a long time coming, but they never gave up and their legacy will speak to future generations. The audience sat for moments in reverent silence in the awe inspiring sanctuary of Arlington.

Fifty years had passed since Albert Whiteside Jr. was Charles' student in twin engine flight training at Tuskegee. In the ensuing years, Whiteside became one of a few black pilots to be certified by the Civil Aeronautics Administration as a commercial pilot in 1946. Rather than leave the country to fly with the "Flying Tigers" in Formosa, he entered a government civil service career, but Whiteside never forgot Charles. When he learned Charles would be a V. I. P. guest at the Air Force Commemorative Banquet at Randolph AFB in Texas, he planned to attend as did his son, formerly a pilot in Vietnam who was now with Federal Express, and his grandson, a member of the junior sector of the Civil Air Patrol. Son and grandson met Charles, who had been so influential in their father's life, and went with him to dedicate a World War II P-51 at Lackland AFB. In congratulatory observations, Whiteside thanked Charles from the heart for "tireless years...(he)...gave to further aviation careers for blacks in and out of the service."

Journalists covering the 50th anniversary of the end of World War II were not silent on the Tuskegee Airmen. In recounting the stories of these aviators, they not only reported history, but corrected it by filling in blank pages from the past. An article in my home town paper related news of a meeting between Charles and John Jones, flight commander in a white bomber group in Italy during the second world war.

The Sunday Messenger reported, "An Athens man who flew 50 bombing missions over enemy territory in World War II broke bread Friday with a member of the Tuskegee Airmen--the fighter group that protected American bombers from German fighters and at the same time made military history.... There is nothing unusual about two World War II veterans sharing a meal and exchanging war stories. But when they were fighting Germans they would never have shared a meal or associated in any way other than their duties demanded."

Other historic divisions were bridged when Charles traveled to Cape Town, South Africa, to meet with veteran pilots from the Republic of South Africa he had not seen since the Korean War.

Traveling for pleasure, he accompanied Yvonne on a scuba diving trip to Grand Caymen Island and experienced the thrill of snorkeling among stingrays. At the ripe age of 76, Charles was forever the adventurer. He was still catching the eye of women, who enjoyed preparing him a meal (although he had become proficient in the kitchen himself) or accompanying him on an outing. While visiting Tesha and her family in Boston, Charles, ever chivalrous, was reputed to be the cause of several church women wearing make up for the first time in years. They inquired when he might return. Virginia Toliver Parsons, widowed after a long marriage, asked a mutual acquaintance about Charles and, learning his whereabouts, contacted him for the first time since they were in high school. Charles visited her on a trip to Denver and they caught up on events of the last sixty years.

A father, grandfather and great grandfather, patriot, aviator, and Tuskegee Airman, Charles continued to be greatly in demand. He openly shared his experiences and others were anxious to learn from his insight and example.

"Have we made progress? Yes. Are things perfect? No. If you're making a difference, what more can you ask!"

Charles' speaking engagements mounted with each passing week. His travels took him from coast to coast and to Africa a second time. Standing in Slave Castle on Gorée Island, Senegal, he held shackles which had imprisoned ancestors forceably brought to America hundreds of years before and he was moved beyond words.

Charles was away when the White House attempted to contact him with an invitation to accompany President Clinton to Japan for the 50th year commemoration of VJ Day. By the time he received the messages and returned the call, he was too late to be included. Plans had gone forward without him. As the song goes "regrets, there've been a few" and for him this was one.

Shortly after, he acquired the means to check his phone messages when traveling. He didn't miss the call when the opportunity to carry the 1996 Olympic Torch was presented several months later. After Richard Hall, a protégé of Charles, left the Air Force, he flew for United Airlines in Atlanta where his wife, LaTessa, took a job for the Olympic Committee. She told Richard they were looking for someone special to carry the torch in D. C. His response was immediate.

"Bingo. We got the man. It has to be Charles McGee."

Looking and feeling fitter than men half his age he was genuinely excited to be a part of the Olympic relay as it passed through Annapolis on its way to Washington, D. C. Waiting for the torch to be passed, Charles spoke to a young boy in the gathering crowd.

"What are you interested in doing some day, son," he asked.

"I don't know," the boy shrugged.

"Why not?"

"Guess cause I never really thought about it," the boy offered.

"And why not. Try (going to) the library this summer. You can learn about far away places and hundreds of things."

The seed planted, Charles accepted the torch and entered the relay.

He added participation in the Olympic torch relay to other experiences that connected him with youth in need of positive role models. Passing the torch among them during speaking engagements in the area and on the road, he would light up their eyes and fire their imaginations, as they too got a chance to touch a part of recent history.

The link between Charles and young people is amazing to witness. In some cases three or more generations stand between, yet a discernible bridge spans their differences, they connect, and some element of essence is exchanged. Even the more hardened and troubled among them are curious. It is as if in him they see a possibility. If he could fight against the odds and succeed, maybe they could too. Like the rest of us, they need real live heroes they can believe in.

That is what Charles is for them and for me.

XIX: Addendum
The Legend and Legacy
1997-2007 Time Line:

- Republican George W. Bush beat democrat Al Gore in a close and contested race to become 43rd President of the United States in January 2001.
- Bush named Gen. Colin L. Powell the first African American to serve as Secretary of State and Condoleezza Rice, also African American, the first woman appointed National Security Advisor.
- On September 11, 2001, an al-Qaeda terrorist attack on the United States killed nearly 3000 people in New York City, Arlington, Virginia and Shanksville, Pennsylvania.
- Forces led by the United States invaded Iraq on March 18, 2003 to disarm the country of weapons of mass destruction, overthrow Saddam Hussein for his support of terrorism and to free the Iraqi people.
- On October 4, 2004 SpaceShipOne made history as it rocketed into space winning the $10 million Ansari X Prize promoting civilian space enterprise and bringing commercial passenger spaceflight one step closer.
- January 2008—Illinois Senator Barack Obama became the first African American to win the Democratic Iowa caucuses, a key stepping stone on the path to the White House.

The legend and legacy of the Tuskegee Airmen continued to grow in the decade after my father's story was initially recorded. A growing recognition of the magnitude and impact of their service stirred interest among aviation enthusiasts, historians and John Q. Public alike. As expressions of admiration and gratitude mushroomed, the forces that first compelled pen to paper gathered anew. And so the saga continues.

On October 14, 1998 in an award ceremony at the Capital Hilton Hotel, Col. Charles McGee received the prestigious Elder Statesman of Aviation Award granted by the National Aeronautic Association (NAA). NAA creators acknowledge that the award, established in

1954 to honor outstanding Americans who have made significant and sustained contributions to aeronautics, is issued very selectively. Nominations are solicited from hundreds of organizations and aviation leaders in the United States and the selections are made by a distinguished committee of leaders from all segments of the aerospace community. Previous winners included notables in the field of aviation such as Eddie Rickenbacker, Jimmy Doolittle, Scott Crossfield, Paul Poberezny and Chuck Yeager.

Charles, usually quite contained when face-to-face with accolades, could not disguise his glee when word of his selection reached him. His delight was still evident when he called to share the news. He wanted to be sure that mention was made in the epilogue of the soon to be published second edition of his biography. In preparing to grant his request I found out why the Elder Statesman award was so special to him.

"It's the nature of the organization," Charles said. "[NAA is] national in scope and the aviators they have recognized are legendary."

A few months later Charles was on hand for the momentous occasion when B.O. Davis Jr. received his 4th star. Davis retired from the Air Force in 1970 as a Lieutenant General (3 stars) and many thought his failure to be promoted to General was once again a consequence of earlier advancement policies for black officers. There was precedence in the Air Force for retrospective recognition when circumstances warranted since others had been given the 4th star in retirement. For several years people worked behind the scenes to gather facts and amass support. Successfully lobbying, this recognition was finally afforded to Davis.

On December 9, 1998 President Bill Clinton pinned a fourth star on Gen. B.O. Davis, Jr. President Clinton described him as "a hero in war, a leader in peace, a pioneer for freedom...." As President of TAI, Charles, along with Woodrow Crockett and several other Airmen, had front row seats to witness the ceremony.

The Airmen had a surprise in store for the President that day. Charles stepped to the podium and asked the President to join him stating, "I have it on good authority that you are not in proper uniform." For a fraction of a second, Clinton appeared startled and it is easy to imagine that his people in charge of protocol were shocked. Charles then invited him to remove his suit jacket and replaced it with the distinctive read blazer of the East Coast Chapter of TAI, making Clinton an honorary Tuskegee Airman.

Until that point in the program the red jacket had been kept out of sight. Dad said he didn't know what the members of the secret service were thinking during this impromptu "coating", but nobody rushed to pull him back and Clinton kept it on for the remainder of the ceremony.

"It was quite an occasion," Charles recalled.

In reflection, Dad observed that the 4th star for Davis was a long time in coming, but a great feeling nonetheless. He was glad the efforts to award it came to fruition when they did. With Davis' health failing any later and the ceremony would not have gone as well. But on that day Davis stood tall and spoke well, every bit the revered leader of Tuskegee Airmen legend.

The following year, Charles celebrated his 80th birthday. Friends and family, along with reporters from different Washington D.C. media gathered to salute him. He told those on hand that he was grateful for a good life and we assured him that it was we who were grateful. The milestone was recognized, however, achieving fourscore had no impact on the pace of activities he resumed immediately thereafter.

A frequent traveler, Charles continued to be in demand on the international as well as domestic scene. He flew to England for speaking engagements at Lakenheath and Mildenhall Air Bases as a part of Black History Month programs, taking the opportunity while there to visit a few outlying locations including the American museum at Duxford.

Charles was also invited back to South Africa, this time at the request of the Chief of the South African Air Force. Although he was certainly treated royally as an honored guest at the annual Air Force gala, his most lasting impression was of the transition that had taken place following the apartheid years. Charles visited a number of bases and schools and witnessed how much was being done for the "majority" population who for so long had been denied education and opportunity.

In his acclaimed work, *The Burden of Memory, the Muse of Forgiveness*, Nobel Laureate in Literature Wole Soyinka explored the question of reconciliation in the aftermath of repression. Soyinka spoke about his ideas at the Great Basin Book Festival that Dad and I attended in Reno, Nevada in September 2000. He did not hold out false hope for an easy course, but offered instead several prerequisites that are essential to social justice once the repression ended: open acknowledgement that a wrong has been perpetrated, sincere public apology by the oppressors, and concrete steps toward reparations—not necessarily of a monetary nature, but essential measures to promote healing for those victimized.

While many descendents of slavery in America feel this country has not yet embraced purposeful steps toward reconciliation, Charles was very interested in the progress he observed in South Africa. A staunch advocate of education himself, he understood and appreciated the importance of special business schools to upgrade the level of training for black Africans to prepare them to enter the mainstream economy.

"It is a big transition and a slow one," Charles observed, "very necessary to bringing disadvantaged people into society and the business world."

Charles' greatest inspiration while in South Africa came during his visit to the Robben Island prison cell where Nelson Mandela spent most of his 27 years of incarceration. Following his release from prison in 1990, Mandela went on to spearhead efforts toward reconciliation in the aftermath of apartheid that lead to a multiracial democracy in South Africa, received the Nobel Peace Prize for this work in 1993, and served from 1994-1999 as its 11th President—the first to be elected in a full participation democracy.

"It was incredible to be where he lived all those years and know that he went on to bring about such a change," Charles said.

Today Mandela is a widely recognized and celebrated elder statesman. In 2007 on his 89th birthday, Mandela launched an initiative called *Global Elders*, a group of 12 wise men and women who share their expertise and guidance in addressing global problems. In the lives he touches, I believe Dad has accepted a similar mission.

On September 11, 2001 Islamic terrorists attacked the United States on its own soil, flying commercial planes into the World Trade Center in New York City. Reeling in shock, the grieving nation mourned the loss of thousands of its citizens, innocent men, women and children in the twin towers once touching the sky, collapsed that day in a sea of dust and rubble.

Most of us recall our whereabouts on this earthshaking day. Charles was in the Houston Intercontinental Airport awaiting a connecting flight to Baltimore Washington Marshall airport following a visit to Houston, where he spoke to the Continental Boeing 777 flight instructors and line check airmen at their annual standards meeting. There was growing commotion around the television monitors in the terminal and Charles along with others pressed in to learn the news. He and other travelers awaiting flights immediately became stranded as the skies above America were closed to all air traffic pending the assessment of present danger.

Like the rest Dad learned of the attack on the Pentagon and the downed airliner in Shanksville, Pennsylvania, and had no notion of the scope of the coordinated atrocities. As confounding as the circumstances were, he had a clear understanding that he needed a way to get home. Securing one of the last rental cars available and a current road map, he started the two day trek overland from Houston to Bethesda staying abreast of developing news and in touch with his family as he traveled.

Wide ranging thoughts were ever present during his road trip. Are additional attacks planned for execution in other unsuspecting locations? Can air space be monitored and made safe for future travel?

Immediate answers were not forthcoming and as days passed the mind-numbing shock subsided. Grief and anger over our loss converged into outrage and President Bush vowed that the criminals who had perpetrated these heinous acts would be hunted down and brought to justice. A course of events was placed into motion that fundamentally altered our way of thinking and behaving as Americans, the ramifications of which have touched us all.

Although not as vocal as the call for justice, there was a more subdued but equally impassioned call for greater understanding. Two weeks following the attacks I delivered a lecture on cultural competency to first year medical students. Following a moment of silence, the ubiquitous expression of national mourning, the opening slide of the lecture read:

TODAY WE UNDERSTAND BETTER THAN EVER BEFORE

THE TERRIBLE PRICE WE PAY WHEN WE ARE UNABLE TO
BRIDGE OUR CULTURAL DIFFERENCES.

Charles' experiences continued to give testimony to the reality
that those bridges can be built. Two short months later he attended
an annual event in Branson, Missouri, billed as America's largest
Veterans Day celebration. In November 2001 the seven-day tribute
to veterans included the historic reunion of the all-white 15th Air
Force Heavy Bomber crews and the all-black Tuskegee Airmen of
the 332nd Fighter Group Squadrons who gave the bombers escort.
The inspiration for the reunion came from World War II B-17 gunner
Dallas McLaughlin whose damaged aircraft was safely escorted
home by Tuskegee Red Tails. Festivities kicked-off with a video-
salute from Tom Brokaw, reporter, news anchor and author of The
Greatest Generation.

Reminiscing took place at Graham Clark Airport around a replica
of Lee Archer's P-51, the Macon Belle, and living history lessons
were presented in the local high school where veterans shared their
stories with students who were generations younger. The enjoyment
of the week-long celebration peaked during the Friday night Hawai-
ian luau. Ed McMahon of Tonight Show fame was at the microphone
to lead off the evening of merriment and musical salutes, but the
show-stopper came when grass skirt-sporting veterans, Charles
among them, took the stage for their rendition of the hula.

*I admit it is a sight that I never thought I'd see—Dad bare-
chested in a hula skirt with one lei around his neck and another tied
on as a head band! But the pictures published in the Veterans Day
edition of the Branson Daily Independent show and tell it all. There
he was—hands waving side to side as he follows the moves of the
scantily clad lead hula dancer. From the look of things, ex-bomber
pilots like to party as much as ex-fighter pilots and that is something
that time had not changed.*

In stark contrast the same edition of the newspaper covered President George Bush's arrival at United Nations Headquarters and his
address to the UN Assembly in which he called for nations to join in
the war on terrorism. "The time for action has arrived," Bush said.
"Nations that support terror are equally guilty of murder and equally
accountable to justice."

In February 2002 Dad and I were invited to the 178th Fighter Wing in Springfield, Ohio, as part of their recognition of Black History Month. Driving along the access road leading to the base, we saw the running digital display that announced his coming and flashed a message of welcome. After saluting, the guard at the gate wanted the honor of shaking his hand. As we toured the base men and women in all areas of operations from supply to security stopped their work and came forward to pay their respects and thank him for his service. The vast majority of the reservists we met that day were white citizens drawn from all walks of life with the common goal of maintaining a high level of preparedness for active duty. I was not expecting that many of them would be well-versed on Dad's history and the show of warmth and admiration that he received from all quarters came as a surprise. Learning more, I was able to attribute it in part to the leadership of the very cordial and gracious base commander, Col. Thomas Pape.

In the afternoon a large group gathered in the base cafeteria to hear Dad's remarks. In introducing him, Commander Pape addressed the crowd and asked that all pilots in the audience stand. He then said for those who had received five or more air medals to remain standing and the majority did so, followed by the same instruction for ten medals at which time several more were seated. By the time he reached more than fifteen only three except Dad remained standing. It was then he said, "The man about to address you has received the service medal an amazing 26 times." The ovation from the crowd swelled then and again at the end of Charles' remarks.

This was one to those special days when your mission in life seems clear. We left the 178th that evening buoyed by good feelings accumulated during our visit and the sense that the connections made there translated into a greater good. People learn to admire and appreciate each other one story at a time; as the story is repeated there is a ripple effect. That day, Dad's story served to inform, enlighten and inspire a new audience and we could hope that through them it would spread to an even wider circle.

On Independence Day, July 4, 2002, Benjamin O. Davis, Jr., Gen, USAF (Ret.) died and Tuskegee Airmen lost the man they considered leader for over 60 years. He was interned in Arlington National Cemetery with full military honors and Charles was among the hundreds of mourners who followed his horse-drawn caisson to his final resting place. Outstanding and ordinary people stood shoulder to shoulder as modern F-15 and F-16 fighters and vintage World War II P-51 Mustangs passed overhead in aerial salute. Several hundred Tuskegee Airmen, now in their seventies and eighties, came from all across the country to bid farewell to the man who led their battles in war and peace. Bill Cosby recognized Gen. Davis' death as "the passing of a major story" in American history.

When his turn to eulogize Davis came, Charles offered these thoughts, "He let us know this was an opportunity [in which] we just could not fail—we were all in the crucible."

For Charles, Davis' legacy was simple: "He worked for the day when we were only Americans and race didn't matter."

Rriveting insight and inspiration can arise even in the midst of most sobering occasions. The McGee family again experienced this first hand when we accompanied Dad to France on the occasion of the 60th anniversary of the D-Day Normandy landing. The journey to come began on May 6, 2004 when Charles received a letter from the French Ambassador to the United States:

Dear Mr. McGee

It is my great pleasure and a great honor to inform you that, by decision of the President of the French Republic, you have been chosen to be named Knight of the Legion of Honor, France's most prestigious award.

This prestigious French distinction is conferred on you by the French Government in recognition for you participation in the liberation of France during the Second World War.

You are part of one hundred American veterans who will be decorated in France on the occasion of the 60th anniversary of the Normandy landing. On the occasion, you will be the guest of the French people and will be invited to attend the celebration of that historic event.

A special flight will leave from Washington DC on June 3rd in the evening and we very much hope you will be able to participate. Just before, at 4 pm the 3rd of June, it is my pleasure to cordially invite you and your guest to at-

tend a reception at the French Embassy, 4101 Reservoir Road, Washington DC that will be held in your honor, to pay tribute to your outstanding actions.

Again, it is a great pleasure for me to convey to you my most sincere and warmest congratulations.

With best regards,

Sincerely,

Jean-David Levitte

That brief missive ushered in a most memorable return to Europe. My sister Yvonne and I were on the same flight to Charles DeGaulle Airport and spent our first night at Hilton Arc de Triomphe before joining brother Ron and family in their hotel with its noteworthy view of the Eiffel Tower. Dad and his guest Ethel Finlay arrived with the official delegation from the US. Dad met Ethel, a World War II pilot herself, on the air show circuit where she shared her experiences as a member of WASP (Women's Air force Service Pilots) who served as ferry pilots, test pilots and training pilots during the war. Due to the size of the group, these special guests of France were assigned accommodations in five deluxe hotels where management and staff had been given the assignment to anticipate their every need and exceed all expectations they may have for five-star treatment.

Dignitaries moved from event to event in police escorted motorcades and it seemed that even the French citizens on the street knew that they were honored guests in their country for the events of the 60th anniversary of D-Day landings. No vestiges of aloofness or signs of political strain were detectible. Matters of cultural labeling, trade balancing and power positioning took a back seat to the mission of conveying an undying gratitude to the country's liberators.

Medal award ceremonies at a historic military academy, an elegant embassy reception, and an evening dinner cruise on the Seine passing the grand landmarks of Paris created a magnificent and surreal adventure. But if all this had been a dream, we awoke the next day to another, boarded trains in the wee hours of the morning, and left Paris heading for the coast to visit Normandy and Arromanches.

The first glimpses of coastal waters and pristine sandy beaches quickly gave way to an extraordinary vista. There is nothing that can prepare you to stand among unending rows of simple white crosses flawlessly aligned in a carpet of green in the cemetery at Colleville-sur-Mer. To gaze across verdant lawn to azure skies and the English Channel knowing that there rested young Americans who did not survive the landing on June 6, 1944 speaks to your soul as nothing before.

The air thickened with excitement as two HMX-1 Marine helicopters landed in a nearby clearing, heralding the arrival of US President George Bush. From my location and the vastness of the crowd and grounds I heard but a few of his prepared remarks. As I strained to see and hear, I could not help but notice the armed guards who were looking not at the podium, but outward towards me. The possibility for violence on this solemn, hallowed ground was not as far removed as I initially imagined.

On the short ride to Arromanches, the escorted caravan of buses passed thru lush countryside, flag-draped cottages and villages with waving French citizens. France's President Jacques Chirac welcomed heads of states from 14 countries, including the Chancellor of Germany attending the D-Day landing anniversary events for the first time, noting that "the wind of Peace, reconciliation and freedom is blowing across Europe, reunited at last." In addition to Germany, America and host country France, other county leaders on hand included Britain (both the Queen and Prime Minister), Canada, Poland, Netherlands, Belgium, Australia, Greece, Luxembourg, Norway, Czechoslovakia, Slovakia, and New Zealand. It is quite a spectacle to witness the arrival and seating of 14 heads of state. I doubt I will ever again see as many heavily-guarded, flag waving, fanfare heralded motorcades or that many gubernatorial dignitaries gathered in one place.

The talks and tributes soon reoriented us to our purpose. In the words of President Chirac:

> *We are gathered here today to remember and pay silent tribute to the fallen on the French soil where on the 6ᵗʰ of June 1944, the hopes of the free world were reborn.*

*After five years of blood and tears, the Allied Landings
in Normandy were to put an end to barbarism in a storm of
steel and fire.
We have not forgotten. We shall never forget.*

The stage for the ceremony at Arromanches was set with the sea as backdrop. In music, film and dance performers paid homage to liberators, nearly 150,000 men who landed on the beaches that day willing to fight and die for freedom. Those in the stands were regaled by a review of multinational armed forces that included marching soldiers, an air show in honor of allied aircraft that liberated the skies of France and a naval armada representing the daring and successful amphibious operations. While US A-10s made the lowest pass of the fly-bys, I had to catch my breath when the Mirages of France released a contrail replica of the tricolor French flag. I imagine that Her Majesty Queen Elizabeth herself, under her signature pastel hat, gave a nod of approval.

Enthralled and spellbound, we watched a recounting of the occupation and liberation of Europe through the interaction of lives performances and larger than life recorded images. The presence of so many heads of state served to give emphasis to the significance of the occasion. They too rose to their feet many times to pay respects to the men and women dead and living whose selfless dedication to duty lead them to fight for the freedom we dearly cherish. As for Charles he was most grateful for the unexpected honor to be among 100 Americans selected for recognition. It was additionally meaningful that arrangements were made for his family to accompany him.

"It's not often that you are recognized by the President of a country and the Minister of Defense, who happened to be a woman," he noted. "French people still realize it [the D-Day landing] meant a return to freedom. The entire event was beautifully done and there were many touching moments to remember."

The trip back home was anything but anticlimactic. Ron, Yvonne and I were together on the same flight, but with a notable variation—Ron was in the cockpit. My brother was check pilot on the Continental 777 flight from Paris to Newark, New Jersey. What a tremendous feeling a pride and confidence to know that your brother is "at the wheel!" Upon landing he treated us to a tour of the cockpit with its innumerable dials and gauges. Dad often compares the thrust of his F-80 jet to one engine on Ron's 777 (a mind boggling 3000 to 90,000 pound difference) as an example of just how far aviation technology has progressed.

The trip to France was truly a captivating and unforgettable experience. While we teased Dad a bit about what to call him now that he was a knight, deciding on Sir Colonel Charles McGee, we never took lightly the lessons we learned from the experience. With Father's Day fast approaching I sat down shortly after returning home to try to capture my thoughts and feelings in a letter to him.

June 14, 2004
Dear Dad,

Home from France, I continue to marvel at the recent ceremonies commemorating the 60th Anniversary of the D-Day Landing and the moving tribute the French people paid you and other veterans of World War II, who fought to free their nation from Nazi tyranny.

Vivid images linger of sitting with my brother and sister in the bright morning sun of the perfect Paris day when you were named a Knight of the Legion of Honor—the stately ceremony at Cour des Invalides in the square of the military academy that Napoleon attended—the red draped steeds of the Calvary—the military band playing the US and French national anthems—the precision marching of troops in review. I am sure General Bonaparte himself would be pleased that the award he commissioned was conveyed to honor those whose service and sacrifice in WORLD WAR II liberated his homeland. Your characteristically humble gratitude did not mask your sheer delight. I could not have been prouder or happier for you.

The predawn train trip north toward Arromanches and Normandy Beach ushered in another amazing day.... President Chirac's words captured the essence of the tribute.

"On 6 June 1944, when the sun set on 'the longest day' and night...fell on France, maimed by years of war and occupation, they held on. They held on to a few acres of sand and soil. But hope was alive again, at last.

Today on the sixth of June, 2004, it is that same hope, that same ideal that we owe to those men whom we shall never forget.

Faced with the dangers of a changing world, let us strive to remain loyal to the legacy, the sacrifice and the message of our fathers. Let us strive to give substance to the humanistic values of respect, justice, dialogue and toler-ance, for which they gave their lives. Let us strive together to build a world of freedom and progress for our children, a world that respects the diversity of individuals, and idea, culture and people."

Dad, I think these words rang true that day because they echoed the values you epitomize and instilled in me, our family and all whom you have touched to give comfort, guid-ance, hope and inspiration. What a fitting way to acknowl-edge your four score and four years of service to God, coun-try and family and others before self!

It is a profound privilege to be your daughter and to have shared in the awesome tributes of the last week. Like the people of France, I convey my love, admiration and deepest gratitude for all you have contributed and the assurance that I will never forget the examples set and lessons learned.

With a full heart and enduring love, I wish you the happi-est of Father's Days

Your devoted daughter

As surviving veterans of the greatest generation shrink in num-bers, there is a growing sense of urgency about capturing their sto-ries and passing them on for the benefit of those who follow. This interest is recognized in military and civilian life in homes, schools, churches, civic groups and political organizations throughout the country. The Air Force recognizes the need by calling their distin-guished pathfinders to the annual Gathering of Eagles at Maxwell Air Force Base in Montgomery Alabama. In this capacity Charles spoke to the 2005 class of field grade officers training for command assignments at Air Command and Staff College along with other dis-tinguished aviators including "The Berlin Candy Bomber" Col. Gail

Halvoren; CW4 Michael Durant, whose experiences were later captured in the book, *Black Hawk Down;* and Brian Binnie, who piloted the first privately manned craft into suborbital space.

"Maxwell recognizes veterans with significant participation,' Charles observed. "To be selected is a singular honor. You get a chance to rub shoulders with some fliers you've only heard about or read about, like Gen. "Davy" Jones of the Doolittle Raiders or Gen. "Tex" Hill who flew with the Flying Tigers in the early years of the war in Indochina."

Charles returned to Maxwell a few years later to a share his experiences and insight with attendees of the Squadron Officers School. While in Montgomery, whenever possible he made the side trip to Tuskegee to check on progress on the restoration of a part of Moton Field, now a 35-acre National Park Service Historic Site. In 1998, Congress passed legislation authorizing $29 million for the Tuskegee Airmen historic site. A portion of that amount had been released to stabilize existing structures, including the red-brick hangar and tower. Work was underway to restore to 1940-42 vintage hangars and outbuildings where primary training took place for Tuskegee Airmen aircrews. An onsite museum already offered visitors a collection of historic materials and artifacts and virtual exhibits about the Tuskegee Airmen's experience. A campaign was launched to raise money to build and maintain a lasting memorial overlooking the restored Moton Field site where someday scenes from the active years of operations during and immediately following WORLD WAR II will be recreated.

"The memorial will be the Tuskegee Airmen's bridge to future generations," Charles emphasized. "The strongest messages for all who visit the memorial will be that the freedoms we enjoy did not come without sacrifice, and that education is essential for all people to develop to their maximum potential. Those of us who remain hope to see it completed in our lifetime. Our task is a mission of highest importance—a very urgent one!"

Another important matter of concern is the future of Tuskegee Airmen, Inc. (TAI).

"We're in transition from a member organization of those who participated [in the experience] to those who want to support the legacy," Charles acknowledged. "There is discussion about how to sustain high membership as the number of originals is getting fewer and fewer. Will those who follow take over the same vision? If not, it has to be replaced with something that will bring and keep folks together."

As a founding member and past president of TAI, Charles continued to devote a good deal of time to the business of the reconceptualizing organization and to what he viewed as the areas of greatest need, namely the foundation in support of youth in aviation and the memorial fundraising efforts.

Beyond TAI activities, annual air shows like the Experimental Aircraft Associations Fly-In at Oshkosh, Wisconsin and Florida's Sun'n Fun offer other chances for large audiences to personally meet and hear from veteran aviators. There were opportunities to speak about past experiences in WORLD WAR II, Korea and Viet Nam and to see old "war birds" (P-40s, P-47s and B-17s and other military aircraft) that were maintained and still flying. Invariably, there were long lines of aviation or history buffs who wanted a book autographed or a print signed or to shake hands with "a part of living history". For Charles the enthusiastic reception and high spirits of these air shows were enjoyable to share.

"Youngsters brought by parents or bussed in as part of a school field trip are eager to listen and to get the signature of someone who was actually there," Charles observed.

Dad and his friend Ethel became regulars on the air show circuit, sometimes pairing to talk about the experience of blacks and women as pilots in WORLD WAR II. While there were common barriers erected by prejudice, there were also differences. Unlike women pilots, the Tuskegee Airmen were ultimately able to receive training, be commissioned and prove themselves in battle. Despite roadblocks to reentry after the war, they were granted veteran benefits. The women who carried out essential functions for the Air Corps were not even afforded a ticket home at the end of their service and veteran's benefits for them were out of the question. Like Tuskegee Airmen, WASPs were eventually recognized (in 1976) for their valuable contributions and women who followed in their footsteps were admitted to flying roles in military and civilian life.

"Women Air Force Service Pilots were treated worse [than us]," Charles lamented. "They served as instructors, ferried planes to and from factories and towed targets for gunnery practice, and when they were no longer needed, they were just sent home."

Charles learned much of the WASP history from Ethel and over time they developed a friendship born of mutual interests in aviation, travel, music and golf.

Even as Charles maintained an active schedule of travel and speaking engagements, he was aware that the creeping elevation in his PSA (Prostate-Specific Antigen) blood work forewarned of recurring cancer. Having successfully battled prostate cancer in the early 1990's, Charles was not shaken by this development and chose to closely monitor it until a more definitive diagnosis was given. That came in fall of 2005 and Charles underwent surgery for colon cancer.

Following the operation, Charles took injections and administered a new oral treatment in lieu of chemotherapy which kept the cancer at bay for a year. However, the need for an immediate second colon surgery came just before his planned trip to Balad, Iraq where he and six other Tuskegee Airmen were to meet airmen of the 332nd Fighter Wing, re-designated as the 332nd Air Expeditionary Wing (AEW) in the Air Force heritage program. Lt. Gen. Walter Buchanan, commander of the US Central Command Air Forces, billed the trip as "linkage between the 'greatest generation' and the 'latest generation'". The Operations Building of the 332 AEW was dedicated in Charles' honor and he looked forward to meeting the men and women of the unit that had honored him, offering encouragement in a time of sacrifice and thanking them for their service. Shortly before the trip Charles, Lee Archer and Herbert Carter were interviewed by the *Mobile Register.*

"I'm proud they're [the airmen] in a unit carrying our name," Charles told reporters. "That's very meaningful from the heritage point of view."

The family felt uneasy about Dad traveling into harms way in a warring Middle East country, but he and his compatriots, having flown in the face of danger before, felt no compunctions about the upcoming visit to Iraq. As fate would have it, his trip was preempted by his second colon cancer surgery.

Charles surgeons apprised him beforehand that they would preserve as much of the colon as possible. Dad awoke to the news that the surgery had gone well. He took this experience in stride as he gained strength and looked forward to a Thanksgiving gathering in Scottsdale, Arizona at the home of his son Ron. So soon after surgery I doubted the trip would be advisable, but to my chagrin Dad, with surgical staples replaced with steri-strips, flew to Arizona less than three weeks later. As he healed and recuperated in the Arizona sunshine at Ron's spacious single-story hacienda, I understood the trip had been the best medicine after all, and within weeks Dad returned to good health and his unrelenting busy schedule.

In Maryland between out-of-town commitments, Charles enjoyed the company of close friends and family in town. Throughout his entire military career it was a luxury to have family nearby and now youngest daughter Yvonne, two grandchildren (Damona Smith Strautmanis and Damon Smith) along with four great-grandchildren were just a stone's throw away. In all, ten grandchildren and nine great-grandchildren were part of the growing family that gathered whenever the occasion permitted—always thankful for the presence of our renowned patriarch. Charles celebrated the landmark achievements of his progeny, on hand when grandson Damon graduated from Harvard Law School and lamenting the conflict that kept him from granddaughter Erin Lanphier's hooding when she received her PhD in Child Psychology. A frequent companion was Mary Louise Mohr, a widow of Tuskegee Airman Dean Mohr. She and Charles enjoyed attending social events and monthly luncheons hosted by others from the Tuskegee group.

In 2006 serious consideration began to emerge about bestowing on Tuskegee Airmen the Congressional Gold Medal. The task of promoting the idea was taken on by Carl Levine, a US senator from Michigan and ranking member of the Senate Armed Services Committee. Charles, along with Col. (Ret) Elmer Jones and Wylie Seldon, worked with the senator to assure the accuracy of the drafted resolution.

"There was quite a bit of concern," Charles recalled, "about [whether or not] only pilots should be the awardees. We pilots could not have done what we did without dedicated support behind us so we opted for all who participated to be recognized."

Recognition of a group with the Congressional Gold Medal is seldom done. While the honor was afforded to the Code Talkers, Native

Americans who worked to transmit secret messages in the Pacific Theater during WORLD WAR II, never before had a group as large as the men and women of the Tuskegee Experience been considered. Nevertheless behind the scenes work began to draft the legislation that would set this precedence.

In the meantime, on February 23, 2006, sixty-three Tuskegee Airmen were awarded honorary degrees from Tuskegee University (formerly Tuskegee Institute) the site that first housed and trained these young men who would go on to aviation accomplishments exceeding all expectations. Charles attended the commencement ceremonies and proudly hung the framed diploma in his home; there for all to see are the words of recognition for a lifetime of achievement:

"By the authority of the Board of Trustees and upon recommendation of the faculty, Tuskegee University hereby confers upon
Charles Edward McGee
The Degree Doctor of Public Service Honoris Causa with all the rights, honors, and privileges appertaining thereto given at Tuskegee, Alabama, the twenty-third day of February Two Thousand and Six"

Along with the Chairman of the Board of Trustees and University Registrar, Tuskegee University President Benjamin Payton affixed his signature to the diploma. Payton had previously welcomed the Airmen in 2002 when they arrived by busloads to celebrate the official opening of the temporary visitor's center at the Tuskegee Airmen National Historic Site on the grounds of Moton Airfield during a side-trip from the National TAI Convention held in Atlanta, Georgia. The site is a partnership of Tuskegee University, the National Park Service and Tuskegee Airmen, Inc. When completed, it will feature fully renovated historical structures, a Visitor Information Center, Archives, a Research Center and facilities for the Tuskegee University Department of Aviation Science.

As for the family, we had a new dilemma. Having previously determined that Sir Col. Charles McGee was the appropriately respectful title, we now pondered the proper addition of Doctor. Sir Col. Dr. Charles McGee is more than a mouthful and will probably seldom be an uttered beyond the playful appellation of an adoring family. Like the article that appeared in the *Daily Dixie* the following day, we applauded the recognition conveyed by Tuskegee University and appreciated too that "Recognition is never too late."

Amidst routine and unforeseen events of daily living, Charles faced the loss of his dear friend Ethyl Finley. Her family asked that he offer the eulogy and once again Charles was called upon to bring words of comfort to others even as he grieved. In this time of sorrow he had the strength and will to characterize the endearing and brave nature of his friend and fellow aviation trailblazer. He spoke of Ethyl the pioneer and determined spirit. He spoke of her work in the WASP program and mentoring young women interested in aviation. He asked those gathered that in honoring Ethyl's memory we:

...not talk about our neighbors, but how we treat our neighbors,
...not talk about the square footage of our house, but how many
    people we welcome into our home,
...not count the clothes in our closet, but how many we have
    helped to clothe,
...not count the number of friends we have, but the number
    to whom we are a friend.

Closing comments brought us full circle to the anonymously authored quote that began his remarks:

"Don't walk in front of me, I might not always follow
Don't walk behind me, I might not always lead
Just walk beside me, and be my friend."

"God's blessings and peace for Ethyl, and for us," Charles concluded.

To every thing there is a season and a time for every purpose under heaven. Charles soon resumed speaking engagements and a demanding travel schedule. Making good on an offer extended at the 2005 TAI National Conference in Orlando, Florida, James Kennedy, Director of the Kennedy Space Center, invited Dad and me to be his guests for the launch of Space Shuttle Discovery the following July. During the pre-launch activities at the Center we learned about the mission of the shuttle program to transport people, spacecraft and equipment to and from the International Space Station (ISS). The specific mission of Discovery's seven crew members was to deliver a multipurpose logistics module and new orbital replacement units to ISS—along with several thousand pounds of new supplies and experiments—and to conduct testing of shuttle inspection and repair hardware.

Excitement built on the day of the launch as buses carried guests to the viewing stands. The enthusiasm we felt was only tempered momentarily by the safety statement we were given. It began with the following caution:

> "Please be advised that hazards are inherent in launching and launch viewing of a Space Shuttle mission. By accepting the invitation to view the launch, you do so with the understanding of potential risk."

This advisory did not come as a total surprise since previously Astronaut Michael Anderson, in addressing a TAI luncheon, told of the incredible thrust which he compared to an explosion that was necessary to lift the shuttle from its launch pad. He went on to say that viewers were initially disappointed to be so far away when first seeing the 184 feet long shuttle perched atop the external tank and rocket boosters two to three miles in the distance. But when the lift-off thrust of 14,685 kilo newtons from each of two solid rocket boosters sends a mushrooming cloud of smoke and debris toward the stands, most viewers become certain that they are much too close.

With all of this in mind, Dad and I sat in the bleachers on that pristine summer day and watched the digital time clock count down. At ten minutes and holding there was talk of weather concerns down range that could compromise a post launch abort should one be necessary. Hard to image looking at the cloudless blue skies overhead until one remembered that within minutes of lift off, the shuttled would be hundreds of miles away.

As it happened, we did not see a launch that day. We learned at a small gathering with Jim Kennedy that evening that the real culprit in the launch delay was an occurrence called "boat in the box". Apparently a seagoing vessel had strayed into the restricted zone where jettisoned tanks and boosters were anticipated to return to earth. It was amazing to learn how many things needed to mesh in order to get a green light for "go" on launch. Two days later all necessary clearances were given and Discovery blasted off on mission STS-121. Dad and I watched it on TV from the comparative safety and comfort of our respective homes. I know he felt privileged for the firsthand look at the new frontier of space aviation and I doubt that either of us would think about the US commitment to space explorations as we had before the visit to Kennedy Space Center.

In the fall of 2006, Yvonne called me to see if I knew that Dad was preparing to take part in an honors program at the Kennedy Center for the Performing Arts, one that he was not at liberty to speak about. Curiosity piqued, now the two of us were left to wonder and speculate, until Dad was finally able to break silence and reveal the news. He was among the veterans paying tribute to honoree Stephen Spielberg in the awards program. Beginning in 1978 Kennedy Center Honors have been given to recognize the lifelong accomplishments and extraordinary talents of the world's most-prestigious artists. Spielberg, for his extraordinary film career much of which brought the most compelling war stories to the big screen, was to receive 2006 honors along with Andrew Lloyd Webber, Dolly Parton, Smokey Robinson and conductor Zubin Mehta.

The task of moderating Spielberg's segment of the ceremonies at the Washington D.C. gala on December 3rd fell to his friend and enthusiastic champion, Tom Hanks. Charles later recalled the warm welcome by Caroline Kennedy, host of the honors program, and how personable Hanks was, things not always anticipated from people of their stature. The rehearsal sessions went well and between takes Hanks chatted with Charles and the other veterans and made a point of thanking them for their service.

At the post event dinner Spielberg talked with the veterans. He commented to Charles that he knew George Lucas of Star Wars fame was planning a movie about the Tuskegee Airmen, words that gave Charles a renewed sense of optimism. Lucas had been interested in the TA story for quite some time, but kept it on the backburner for years during the making of the Star Wars Trilogy.

"The fact that Spielberg mentioned it meant it was moving forward," Charles enthused.

CBS televised the event later in the month during the Christmas holidays. The family gathered around the TV set for the awards show and his children and grandchildren beamed while great grandchildren squealed with delight to see "Papa Gee" take center stage at Kennedy Center on prime time national television. Not only family, but friends from far and wide also called in the days that followed to say, "I saw you on TV."

"It was a good feeling to be selected to represent veterans around the country," Charles reflected. "A singular honor indeed."

Behind the scenes inside the Washington DC beltway, the quest for the Congressional Gold Medal moved forward. With Senator Carl Levin's leadership the Senate was first to act. Congressman Charles Rangle picked up the mantel for the House of Representatives. He had been a champion for the program, what it stood for and what it meant. Both the Senate and House Bill passed unanimously and the act was signed by President Bush. Still there were several tasks to accomplish before the medals could be awarded. Time was needed to design and produce them. The original was to reside in the Smithsonian Institution and replicas would be struck for some 300 recipients who were expected to attend the award ceremony in the Rotunda of the Capitol, and a small number of others unable to make the trip to Washington who would attend ceremonies at other locations. A flurry of planning activities was set in motion and the date for the award selected.

A fuller appreciation of the magnitude of the honor can be gleaned from understanding how the conveyers view the award. The following description appeared in program materials.

> "The Congressional Gold Medal is the most distin-guished award bestowed by the United States Congress. It is the nation's top civilian award presented to those individuals that embody the best quality in America's heritage. Before it can be awarded, legislation must be approved by Congress and signed into law by the President. Congress first awarded the Congressional Gold Medal to George Washington in 1776."

It was this elite company that the Tuskegee Airmen joined. The official letter of invitation from Speaker of the House Nancy Pelosi stating that "The Congress of the United States requests the honor of your presence...." Thus began a series of events and the myriad of interviews that played out over the course of the year and into 2008.

The day for the conveyance of the Congressional Gold Medal to Charles and other surviving Tuskegee Airmen was March 29, 2007. It was a crisp clear day that aptly spoke to the transition from winter to spring. The white dome of the Capitol rising in a brilliant blue sky provided a picture perfect backdrop for those convening. Dad, Ron and I parked at Union Station and made the short walk to Capitol Hill. Yvonne, now an editor for the Pentagon Channel, was among the news teams setting up to cover the event. Dad had agreed to a series of interviews in the days leading up to the award ceremony and the incessant use of his voice left him a bit hoarse—a concern since he was expected to make remarks during the program. Nevertheless he was amenable when a reporter asked to meet him in front of the State House for yet another comment for the record and when dubbed to speak by telephone with a British Broadcasting Company (BBC) reporter covering the event from London.

Slowly the gathering crowd made its way to the staging area and from there guests converged on the Rotunda in numbers far greater than anticipated. The standing room only crush continued to swell as we awaited the entrance of the honorees. Several times audience members were asked to give up seats for a Tuskegee Airman's widow or to move to an overflow anteroom if not a Rotunda ticket holder. The momentous nature of the occasion made most reluctant to lose a good vantage point, but fortunately chivalry resulted in accommodation.

And finally the moment came that had been a lifetime in the making. Distinguished members of the platform entered. People stretched and strained to see Colin Powell or Charlie Rangle among others—and then Pelosi and finally the President of the United States who took his seat soon to rise for the entrance of the Tuskegee Airmen. The room was charged with excitement and the ovation grew thunderous as they moved though the aisles. Some like Charles were erect and surefooted; others more bowed and lumbering and still others made their way with assistance or in wheelchairs. What mattered was not how surely they moved, only how far they had come.

The accolades began. They were poignant and eloquent and

sometime humorous but no matter how glowing they never seemed overblown or inflated in comparison to the achievements they recounted. There are times when words can not express the full extent of an emotional experience. They did not fail that day; nor did the accompanying actions which also spoke volumes.

The most memorable point of the ceremony for Charles was when President Bush said, "… I would like to offer a gesture to help atone for all the unreturned salutes and unforgivable indignities. And so, on behalf of the office I hold, and a country that honors you, I salute you for the service to the United States of America." Tuskegee Airmen rose to their feet, assisting those in wheelchairs to stand, to receive and return the salute—an action which brought tears to the eyes of the President as well as those in attendance.

"The Commander-in-Chief saluted us for what our accomplishments meant to the country—for all Americans," Charles reflected.

> *Those of us in attendance were equally moved. Bush spoke about being raised by a World War II veteran and of the difficulties and sacrifices made by his father and fellow airmen. Yet he acknowledged that their plight was not as great as that of the Tuskegee Airmen.*

> *"…they never had the burden of having their every mission, their every success, their every failure viewed through the color of their skin. Nobody told them they were a credit to their race. Nobody refused to return their salutes. Nobody expected them to bear the daily humiliations while wearing the uniform of their country."*

> *He went on to observe that the "Tuskegee Airmen helped win a war, and you helped change our nation for the better. Yours is the story of the human spirit, and it ends like all great stories do—with wisdom and lessons and hope for tomorrow. And the medal that we confer today means that we're doing a small part to ensure that your story will be told and honored for generations to come."*

His words rang true for those who were of the experience and to their descendents who had preserved and cherished the heritage unaided for so long. Now, the leader of the free world spoke of the past indignities and humiliations acknowledging them for all to hear. We hung on every world, punctuating truths with affirmations and applause. And when we didn't know it could be more meaningful, President Bush did something most unexpected—he offered on behalf of the country his salute as a gesture of atonement. Most amazingly, there it was, one—and perhaps two—of Wole Soyinka's prerequisites for social justice that are essential to reconciliation—an open acknowledgement that a wrong has been perpetrated and a sincere public gesture of amends. A simple act with the power to promote healing!

So much to absorb and take in not only for the moment, but to preserve for future days. Maybe one when burdens weigh heavily and sweet recall offers perspective and solace. Even better on a day for recounting the blessings of a good life. The day that the Tuskegee Airmen received the Congressional Gold Medal will surely be on the list and in a prominent place.

What more can be said about the impact of a worthy life? As a guardian of the heritage I sometimes travel and speak on behalf of the Tuskegee Airmen. When asked what motivated me to capture in print the essence of my father's experiences, the answer I share is embodied in concepts of history, heroes, healing and hope.

For too long the contributions of the Tuskegee Airmen were obscured at best and in some cases consciously distorted in the annals of history. Time had come to set the record straight. Thankfully the silence has been broken on many fronts and more and more hands rise when audiences are asked who among them knows the story of the Tuskegee Airmen.

A hero is defined as a person admired by virtue of accomplishments and character, particularly in the face of adversity. It is admirable and inspiring to overcome hardships and go on to make significant contributions; however, modern day heroes too often fall short as acts of poor judgment and questionable character come to light. Not so for Charles and other Tuskegee Airmen who are unquestionably role models from the "Greatest Generation". By any definition they qualify as bona fide heroes worthy of emulation.

In the struggle for equal justice and racial healing, Dad's story serves to inform, enlighten and inspire new and widening circles of people. For more than three centuries the stories that divided the races in this country were propagated and emphasized to keep barriers erected. They were fabrications about character and capability that allowed whites to subjugate blacks without the burden of guilt; tales that allowed blacks to preserve dignity and self worth by viewing subjugation as a moral deficiency in whites. A century and a half ago we began the effort to rewrite these well-rehearsed scripts and a half century ago to remove legal barriers and ensure everyone the full rights of citizenship. The dialogue of racial healing is still new in comparison to the dialogue of division; the stories that bring us together are too few. Dad's is one for the record.

Hope is the driving force of change. Born of the vision of a better day, it compelled the young men and women who became Tuskegee Airmen to leave behind their known worlds and to navigate hostile territory. It was the hope that they could be instruments of change that would usher in that new day. And by virtue of their success that hope swells again in generations that follow.

Charles' message to young people is straightforward: set challenging goals, work hard, never give up and help others along the way. In schools, churches and civic groups he asks, "will a young man or woman listening in the audience here today be on a mission to Mars in the year 2030?" Some look around as they consider the question while others are still and reflective. He acknowledges that it won't be him; but why not one of them. It is another opportunity to motivate young people living in a different world to become leaders for tomorrow.

"They are living in an era of greater diversity and commanding technology with yet uncertain values," Charles reflects. "Citizens of tomorrow need to prepare themselves to keep American strong and prosperous if we are to sustain the freedom we enjoy."

What better way for them to achieve that purpose than by instilling in them the lessons learned from the Tuskegee Airmen.

As for Charles, at eighty-eight the adventures and opportunities to inspire and motivate continued. "Top secret" orders arrived from Lee Lauderback of the Stallion 51 Corporation, a clever plan for inviting

Charles to be one of 51 living Legends to be honored at the Gathering of Mustangs and Legends where tribute would also be paid to the revered P-51 Mustang. By final count 77 of the venerable aircraft were on hand along with the Thunderbirds, F-15s, F-16s, and F-22 Raptors. Heritage flights of these current fighters in formation with vintage fighters thrilled crowds estimated at 150,000 that gathered at Rickenbacker International Airport in Columbus, Ohio, the location chosen to host the gathering. This site was particularly meaningful to Charles because Rickenbacker opened in 1942 as Lockbourne Army Air Base and served for a time as home to the 332nd Fighter Wing of the Tuskegee Airmen.

When asked what is so special about the P-51, Charles responded immediately.

"It's a joy to fly," he asserts. "Wonderful from the ground to 35,000 feet. Speed, range and control capability showed it to be a marvelous aircraft. Particularly with the Rolls Royce Merlin engine. You know that sound [when you hear it] every time!"

From Columbus, Charles and son Ron proceeded to Elmendorf Air Force Base near Anchorage, Alaska for the 477th Fighter Group Activation Ceremony. As part of the heritage preservation initiative, the former bomber group of Tuskegee Airmen was activated and re-designated as the Air Force Reserve Command's first F-22A Raptor Fighter Group. In his letter of invitation, Commander Eric Overturf offered these observations.

"Dating back to the World War II era, these units [477th Fighter Group and 302nd Fighter Squadron] were…[assigned to] the Tuskegee Airmen, arguably the most professional and proficient aviators in the Army Air Corps. Their record has stood the test of time as the standard for excellence. We look forward to demonstrating the pride we have in the 477th Fighter Group heritage through continued excellence in honor of the great Airmen who went before us."

Before leaving Elmendorf, Charles was made honorary Commander of the 302nd Fighter Squadron, a distinction he accepted with the utmost pride and humility.

And what of this record of the Tuskegee Airmen that has "stood the test of time"? Of late, TAI national historian William Holton as well as another Air Force historian Daniel Haulman, Chief of the Organizational Histories Branch of the Air Force Historical Research

Agency, investigated questions about the veracity of the claim of never loosing a bomber under the escort of Tuskegee Airmen to an enemy fighter. They concurred that several losses are recorded in mission records and research continues to corroborate and validate the information. It is difficult to precisely determine if a loss was due to enemy fighters or other causes and where the loss occurred.

Some within the TAI organization view this development as a threat that will work to undermine the recognized contributions of the Tuskegee Airmen. Charles fears not.

"No matter how you look at it, the Tuskegee Airmen have an unequaled record," Charles observed. "If a few losses are confirmed, that will still be the case. We should take the lead in discovering and reporting the truth. Facts and our achievements will continue to speak for themselves."

Clarence Anderegg, Director of the Air Force Museum Histories, Policies and Programs agreed with Charles. Holton recalled Anderegg's comments during an address to the Executive Committee Meeting of the TAI Board in August 2007. He noted that resources of his division were dedicated to documentation of current missions and no longer being spent in clarifying issues of [World War II] history. However he went on to say that "In my opinion, it [performance of the 332nd] was an extraordinarily good record."

During a TAI convention, my sister Yvonne asked me to imagine what the organization will be like in 10 years. It was a simple request that was riveting in its effect. The mind struggles when asked to go where it does not wish to venture—to the time when the voices of the Tuskegee Airmen are quieted with only echoes to remind us of their strength and wisdom. But even in that dark place of loss and angst a deeper understanding took hold and grew to become a glimmer then beacon of hope. As long as there are guardians of the heritage, the story will be told, the heroes will be honored, healing will continue and hope will live on.

That night a tribute was born as I feverishly worked to write and edit verse after verse. As dawn broke following sleepless hours I looked at the words before me fully understanding that I was the mere vehicle of their expression. They were of my hand but inspired beyond me; I felt grateful to be the means of their conveyance.

There is peace that comes with greater understanding. With each recitation of this and other tributes that have been offered, the legend will come alive again. As long as there are guardians of the heritage the legacy of the Tuskegee Airmen will speak to the best aspects of the human spirit for generations to come.

Tuskegee Airmen:
A Tribute from Guardians of the Heritage

Their lives before Tuskegee were known to but a few
A Negro son in a racist land, living out of view
Amid so many faces, theirs may have gone unseen
But for a fateful decision to pursue a far off dream.

They left behind the places they knew, the city streets and country roads
Converging from all walks of life to take the path they chose
Their reasons were as varied as past lives and their hue
Yet destined to come together, a common lot they drew

An inner voice guided as they set their standards high
These young black men in a world of strife, determined and eager to fly
In their heads there was a vision of a new and brighter day
In their hearts a faith their service would help to forge the way

They set out on a course that tested mind, body and spirit
The challenge was immense, but they were steadfast and committed
Believing in themselves and the worthiness of the prize
They proved equal to the rigors and gained access to the skies

As pilots they served America, when their chance was earned
For love of country they paid a price, war's harshest lessons learned
They fought on despite loss and hardship, in the face of bigotry and hate
Becoming guardians of hostile skies and masters of their fate

Ten men below worked tirelessly for each fighter overhead
And in time opposition changed to respect, as word of their valor spread
Not so for black bombers stateside, trapped in an endless stall
Denied their rights, some were jailed, and none would answer the combat call

War heroes came home when the battle ended with victory in hand
But Tuskegee Airmen were shunned and rejected,
    still seen as less than their fellow man
Once more they would not be denied, their will too strong to fail
And they fought on for justice and democracy to prevail

With their unrelenting efforts resistance began to yield
Critics forced to step aside, opportunity at last revealed
Finally the chance they fought for was extended to a few
Then others and then more, and from there the numbers grew

While the rest is part of history, their work is not complete
Until promise is reality, we have a charge to keep
Inspired by their example, we strive for higher ground
And from their noble legacy our needed strength is found

Some ask how they could serve and die for such a thankless land
The answer is apparent from their shoulders where we stand
They fought against oppression, freedom the victory to be won
For in the American tradition, they are truly native sons

We are in awe of mortal men who rise to give their best
To make this world a better place before they take their rest
We honor and revere them for their lives of dedication
Tuskegee Airmen who dared to dream, whose courage changed a nation.

First Period
PHOTOS

1. The Charles Allen McGee family circa 1911. Back (l. to r.)
Richard, Ruth, Lewis (Charles' father), Cecilia and Grace. Front
(l. to r.) Charles Allen, Gay Ruth, and Charles Franklin.

2. Lewis with wife Ruth and
Lewis Jr. in 1917.

3. The McGee children: Ruth M.,
Charles E. and Lewis Jr. standing.

4. Frances E. with brother
Leonard Nelson circa 1924.

5. Frances E. with best friend
Stella Baines (Nelson).

6. The marriage of Charles and Frances, October 17, 1942.

7. The Class of 43-F, Tuskegee Army Air Field, SE Flying Training Command, June 1943 (Charles front row 4th from the right).

8. World War II: Charles with his P-51C "Kitten".

9. Frances "Kitten" at home during World War II.

10. Charles in Italy during World War II.

Second Period
PHOTOS

11. The growing family: Captain McGee with
Frances, son Ronald and daughter Charlene.

12. The 67th Fighter Bomber Squadron pilots
in Korea (Charles seated on the right).

13. Korean War pilots ready to embark on a mission (Charles 2nd from left)

14. Mission accomplished: 7000th sortie by 18th Fighter Group.

15. Charles and crew with P-51D "Kitten" in Korea. (l. to r.) T/SGT Quinn, Major McGee, T/SGT Laughrun, and T/SGT R. Tomasini.

16. Gen. Partridge, CO 5th Air Force, pins Distinguished Flying Cross on Major McGee, Chinhae, Korea, January 23, 1951.

17. The boys of the 44th Fighter Squadron
(Charles, front row, sixth from right).

18. Charles gives Henry Luce,
editor of *Time-Life* Magazine,
a jet airplane flight in T-33.

19. Veteran pilots of Korea
in the 44th FBS in front of F-80
(Charles standing 2nd from left.)

20. Winter Survival Training, Spokane, WA
(Charles squatting second from right).

21. Charles receives congratulatory fire truck
shower after final mission (RF-4C in background).

22. Vietnam medal award
ceremony, Heidelberg, Germany.

23. Charles swears in son Ronald
as 2nd LT in the U.S. Air Force.

24. General Stony presents
Charles with retirement
certificate, January 1973.

25. Charles, Base and Wing Co.,
Richards-Gebaur AFB, Missouri.

Third Period
PHOTOS

26. Charles in retirement.

27. The McGee's at a reunion in

28. Frances in retirement.

29. Charles and Frances with first great grandson, Michael Devon Myers.

30. Charles receives Noel Parrish Award, from Dr. Florence Parrish, 1988 TAI Convention (COL Harry Sheppard seated).

31. Charles welcomes first Ph.D. into the family, daughter Charlene.

32. Dedication, Tuskegee Airmen memorial statue, Air Force Academy, Colorado Springs, with Major General Lucius Theus.

33. Charles in salute to veterans parade, Columbia, Missouri, 1996.

34. Charles introduces children to aviation.

35. Holding shackles used in the slave trade, Goree Island, Senegal (West Africa), 1996.

36. Carrying the Olympic Torch en-route to games in Atlanta, 1996.

37. Charles and LT. Gen. Lester Lyles, en-assisted by honor guard, laying wreath

38. Swimming with stingrays in the Grand Cayman Islands, 1996.

39. With grandchildren, (l. to r.) Kelsey, Charon, and Aidan
and great grandchildren Michael Damani, Charles Darrien, and
Michael Devon.

40. In reflection.
(Photo courtesy of Gary J. Kirksy)

Fourth Period
PHOTOS

41. President Bill Clinton just prior to becoming an honorary Tuskegee Airman at B.O. Davis' Four-star ceremony. Left to right: B.O. Davis, Howard Baugh, President Clinton, Woodrow, Crockett and Charles McGee.

42. Charles becomes a Knight in the French Legion of Honor on the 60th anniversary of D-day, June 2004.

43. Last resting place for America's fallen soldiers on D-day, Colleville-Sur-Mer, France

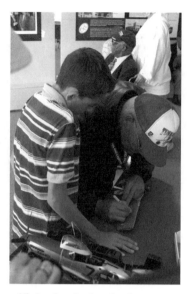

44. Charles at Gathering of Eagles Command and Staff College.

45. An inspiration for the next generation. Charles signs a Model P-51 at the Mustang and Legends gathering in Columbus, Ohio.

46. Charles instructs from the cockpit of a P-51 Mustang to an attentive pupil, daughter, Charlene.

47.Charles by Princess Elizabeth P-51 at Mustangs and Legends.

48. Charles with Major Paul "Max" Moga demonstration pilot, at Mustang and Legends.

49. Charles present and past. A F-22 larger than life banner honoring him at Mustangs and Legends.

50. Charles at conveyance of Congressional Gold Medal March 29, 2007. Left to right: President George W. Bush, Speaker Nancy Pelosi, Charles and Lee Archer.

51. Charles is congratulated following the Gold Medal Ceremony by Illinois Senators Dick Durbin (left) and Barack Obama (center).

52. Charles after the Congressional Gold Medal Ceremony with his proud children (left to right) Ron, Charlene and Yvonne.

53. Charles with grandchildren and great grandchildren; a role model for future generations.

TRIBUTES

"...Charles (Colonel McGee) has influenced my life in many ways". He was the first black Wing Commander at this base (Richards-Gebaur AFB)."

John "Jack" Adams
Lt. Col. USAF (Ret.)

"He was a wonderful leader, a great pilot and a dedicated patriot. I have considered it as a blessing that I was able to serve under him and observe his leadership in the formative years of my career."

Frank Borman
Astronaut

"After fighting in World War II, Col. Chuck McGee went on to fly and fight in Korea and in Vietnam. He racked up the highest three-war total of fighter missions of any Air Force aviator— 409 missions"....An American hero and an Air Force legend.

Ronald R. Fogleman
General, Chief of Staff, USAF

"He had been my inspiration to become a pilot since my days as a cadet at the Air Force Academy. Prior to that...I had fallen for the myth black people could not aspire to such unique goals. I am now a Boeing 767 pilot for United Airlines and active in Tuskegee Airmen, Inc.....Col. McGee carried the Olympic Torch on its trek to Atlanta and the start of the Centennial Olympic Games.... (and) carried 'The Torch' for many of us once again."

Richard P. Hall
Pilot, United Airlines

"He really cares and he has the ability to talk with anyone at any time on any subject.... He's a good listener also.... His integrity is commendable. He is a man of God and he loves his family very much."

Rubye Hatchett
Tuskegee Airmen, Inc.
Heart of America Chapter

"I never met a finer gentleman in my Air Force career. I'm proud to be able to say that 'Chuck' McGee was my friend and fellow fighter pilot."

Edward F. Hodges
Fighter Pilot

"Just received (word) about the book on Charles McGee. A real gentleman and outstanding fighter pilot and leader."

Col. Bill E. Myers
Fighter Pilot

"...Charles is a gentleman in all respects on all occasions."

George W. Parker
Major, USAF (Ret.)

"I always felt very honored to be counted among...(Charles and Frances') friends. (Charles) is very special and helped look out for my welfare in time of need. He not only took his military mission so serious, but also the human side of his people....he did love to jitterbug....a very remarkable man!!!"

Erika B. "Ricky" Parrish
USAF Family Friend

"He (Charles) is such a fine example of a human being in our time...."

Barbara J. Peter, R. N.
USAF Dependent

"I certainly remember the reception at Richards-Gebaur (AFB) honoring the Tuskegee Airmen. I was very happy when he (Charles) was ...to receive two standing ovations."

William A. Pollock
Lt. Col. USAF (Ret.)

"It has been said an organization ... 'takes' on the character of its leader..... Never did he (the flight scheduling officer) have any trouble getting crews to fly some of our most hazardous missions. I attribute this attitude to the example and leadership of our C.O. (commanding officer) Charles McGee."

Ray Renfro
Col. USAF (Ret.)

"He is my mentor and ...always treated me with respect and compassion. Surely my life has been enriched by knowing Charles....a man of high morals...(who) set his goals high."

Dr. Jerry A. Taylor
Family Friend

"Col. McGee...I...commend you on the many years of faithful service which you have given to the promotion of aviation for blacks IN and OUT of military service."

Albert Whiteside, Jr.
Captain USAF (Ret.)
Tuskegee Airman (Class 45E)

Resources

1. Benson, L. *A brief History of the USAF: Golden legacy, boundless future.* January 1, 1997 (Updated June 15, 1998). DSN 487-4685, Randolph AFB, TX.

2. *Civil Rights Timeline.* (1998). Seattle Times. Www.seattletimes.com/mlk/movement/Seatimeline. html.

3. *Conflict in Southeast Asia: 1961-1973.* Vietnam History Gallery. Www.wpafb.af.mil/museum/history/vietnam/prolog.htm.

4. Cooper, C. & Cooper, A. (1996). Tuskegee's Heroes. Motorbooks International. Osceola, WI.

5. Coren, M. (2004). Commercial space travel next leap for mankind? Private manned flight test may launch new era in aviation accessed at
http://www.cnn.com/2004/TECH/space/06/18/ssone.fl
ight.history/index.html on February 1, 2008.

6. Coren, M. (2004). SpaceShipOne captures X Prize: Privately funded craft reaches altitude requirement accessed at
http://www.cnn.com/2004/TECH/space/10/04/spaceshipone.attempt.c
nn/index.html on February 1, 2008.

7. Davis, Jr., B. (1991). *An autobiography: Benjamin O. Davis, Jr., American.* Smithsonian. Washington, DC.

8. Fischer, Bill (2007). Gathering of Mustangs and Legends Is an Event for the Ages. *Warbirds.* 30(8), p26-30.

9. Fogleman, R. *Tuskegee Airman: Breaking the myths.* Delivered at the Tuskegee Airmen Convention, Atlanta, GA., August 12, 1995.

10. Francis, Charles. (1997). *The Tuskegee Airmen: The Men Who Changed a Nation.* 4th Edition, Edited, Revised, Up-Dated and Enlarged by COL Adolph Caso. (First book, *Tuskegee Airmen* first published in 1955), Branden Publishing Company. Boston, MA.

11. Guttman, J. (1999). Charles McGee: Tuskegee and Beyond. Aviation History. March 1999, 38-44,67.

12. Harris, J. (1996). The Tuskegee Airmen: Black heroes of World War II. Dillon Press. Parsippany, NJ.

13. Kanner, G. (1967). Korean War (1950-1953). Collier's Encyclopedia. 14, 168-172.

14. Mandela, N. (1994). Long walk to freedom: The Autobiography of Nelson Mandela. Little, Brown and Company, Ltd. Boston, MA.

15. McKissack, P. & McKissack, F. (1995). Red-Tail Angels: The story of the Tuskegee Airmen of World War II. Walker and Company. New York, NY.

16. McNeil, A. (1996). Aim High. PONY. 42(7), 10-12.

17. National Aeronautic Association Website: www.air-boyne.com/naa.htm on 9/29/07 and www.naa. aero/html.awards/index.cfm?cmid=63 on 3/29/07.

18. Phelps, J. (1991). *American's first black four-star general: Chappie, the life and times of Daniel James, Jr.* Presidio. Novato, CA.

19. Rose, R. (1976). *Lonely Eagles.* Tuskegee Airmen, Inc., Los Angeles Chapter. Los Angeles, CA.

20. Sandler, S. (1992). *Segregated Skies: All-Black Combat Squadrons of WW II.* Smithsonian Institution Press. Washington, DC.

21. Smith, G. (1997). *Chief.* American Legacy. 3(2), 6-7.

22. Wilkinson, B. (1997). *The civil rights movement: An illustrated history.* Crescent Books. New York, NY.

23. On-line information regarding The Burden of Memory, the Muse of Forgiveness by Wole Soyinka accessed at: http://books.google.com/books?id=AEFndpEmhVwC&pg=PP1&dq=inauthor:Wole+inauthor:Soyinka&sig=erR253IR-LJEOsDNgBkGmbndikU

24. On-line information regard Nelson Mandela accessed at: http://en.wikipedia.org/wiki/Nelson_Mandela

25. On lineInformation on the Tuskegee Airmen National Historic Site accessed at Black Issues in Higher Education, 12 Spt 2002, ttp://findarticles.com/p/articles/mi_m0DXK/is_15_19/ai_92082294

26. On-line information accessed from the Web site of Daily Dixie at hppt://www.daily Dixie.com/

27. On-line information regarding the invasion of Iraq accessed at http://en.wikipedia.org/wiki/2003_invasion_of_Iraq

ABOUT THE BOOK:

Colonel Charles E. McGee fought in World War II, in Korea, and in Vietnam. He holds the record for the highest three-war total of fighter combat missions of any pilot in U.S. Air Force history.

His military service began as one of the Tuskegee Airmen in the 332nd, famed pioneers who fought racial prejudices to fly and fight for their country in World War II. These men, who trained hard and fought bravely for their country, returned home to find attitudes unchanged and joined in another battle to desegregate the armed services. Their strategy, of peaceful but persistent confrontation challenging racial barriers in the military, broadened the foundation for the civil rights movement.

Colonel McGee went on to serve in leadership and command positions in war and in peace flying fighter missions in Korea and Vietnam. In his remarkable military career, he earned the Legion of Merit with Cluster, three Distinguished Flying Crosses, the Bronze Star and the Air Medal—an amazing twenty-five times.

After retiring from the Air Force, Colonel McGee devoted himself to numerous good causes, particularly those encouraging young people to achieve. Twice he was chosen to lead Tuskegee Airmen, Inc serving two separate terms as president of the international association. For distinguished dedication to country and continuous selfless hours of service in the interest of aviation, Colonel McGee was honored by the National Aeronautic Association, receiving its prestigious recognition as Elder Statesman of Aviation. On March 29, 2007 he and other surviving Tuskegee Airmen were awarded the Congressional Gold Medal, the most distinguished award bestowed by the United States Congress.

Too often African American men in America are not portrayed as heroes. In tribute to the many unheralded fathers, husbands, sons, and brothers leading exemplary lives, Colonel McGee's inspiring story is now being told.

ABOUT THE AUTHOR:

Charlene Smith and her husband William divide their time between homes in Athens, Ohio, and Annapolis, Maryland. A tribute to belief in the value of education, the family has twelve college degrees among them (and still counting). Dr. Smith earned a bachelor degree in Education (University of Illinois), masters degree in Health Services Administration (U. of I. Springfield) and Ph.D. in Communication from Ohio University. In Athens, she continues affiliation with Ohio University following years of service in progressive administrative and faculty appointments. In Annapolis she enjoys the ambience of Chesapeake Bay life and close connections with nearby family including father, Charles McGee.

Index